To Lily and J...

to mark your
Ruby Wedding

17th April, 1977.

From Mary and ...

"Cheerio Frank Cheerio Everybody"

"Cheerio Frank Cheerio Everybody"

THE GARDENING WORLD OF FRED STREETER

By Frank Hennig

Line drawings by Barbara Law

Angus and Robertson · Publishers

Angus & Robertson · Publishers
London · Sydney · Melbourne · Singapore · Manila

First published by Angus & Robertson (U.K.) Ltd 1976
Copyright © Frank Hennig 1976

ISBN 0 207 95711 8

Photoset, printed and bound
in Great Britain by
REDWOOD BURN LIMITED
Trowbridge & Esher

Contents

Foreword

It was impossible not to respect and admire Fred Streeter. His qualities were self-evident, and he shared them so generously with others. As a gardener he was, of course, without rival; as a man his immense kindness and wisdom were an inspiration to all who knew him. Now Frank Hennig, one of those who knew him best, has produced this valuable and sensitive account of Fred Streeter and his world. Mr. Hennig's subject emerges as the most delightful and gentle of men, and the portrait is therefore a true one. Like many who live close to the land, Fred Streeter possessed an outlook on life that was a wonderful combination of wisdom, acumen and good humour. He is sorely missed by all who were privileged to share his thoughts and receive his advice: if this book reminds them of him, and introduces him to others, it will have served an excellent purpose.

The Rt. Hon. Lord Egremont

Preface

In a lifetime of ninety-eight years, Fred Streeter never had a *real* holiday. Even a visit to Paris in the Spring soon found him longing for home and heading back to his English Country Garden.

His philosophy was simple. If you are devoted to your work, you'll find little relaxation in leaving it – even if only for a week or two. And he applied that philosophy both to his gardening and his broadcasting; no sooner would we complete one broadcast that he would be turning his mind to the topic for next week's discussion.

The Frank-and-Fred broadcasting partnership was only established during the last nine years of Fred's life. In a sense it was a postscript to his career. Yet it kept him very much 'the voice of gardening' to the last, and he was one of those rare people who was better known and had a wider circle of friends in his 90's than at any other time in his life.

He was not only a great gardener. He was a first-rate showman too, with a sense of occasion that stayed with him to his final recorded broadcast on the day he died. It was on All Saints Day 1975. He spoke of the roses he loved so well. And his last words on the air were simply – "Cheerio Frank. Cheerio everybody. Old Fred Streeter will keep pegging away!"

I

"Sometimes we try to be a bit too clever in this world, Frank. Take the poor old gardener who's plagued by blackfly. He'll spend a small fortune on sprays and things when all he need do is take a little soil from the bottom of the plant and sprinkle it like powder all over those blessed blackfly. That'll finish them off ... it gets in their teeth you know!"

Fred Streeter was right. Two days after that broadcast in the summer of 1974 I put his treatment to the test for a particularly nasty attack of blackfly on my runner beans. Results were slow in coming – but come they did, for the blackfly gradually fell from the plants like defeated jungle warriors dropping from the trees. Fred had scored another garden victory and my canister of insecticide remained unopened in the shed.

Close on forty years earlier, one Sunday afternoon in 1935, Fred had made his first broadcast. Some broadcasters launch themselves into radio from a pinnacle of success. Maybe they make some, politically outrageous comment that has the Nation rocking on its heels; or perhaps they have performed with such disarming wit at the microphone that, long before the programme is over, we know we'll be hearing from them time and time again.

Fred trod a very different path to fame. His first topic on the air was the care and cultivation of peas and runner beans. He spoke for only ten minutes, yet listeners were quick to realise that here was something refreshingly new in the world of wireless – a broadcaster who could talk about gardening in a way that made it sound like high adventure. No deep technicalities from Fred. No bland assumptions that we were all on nodding terms with every jaw-cracking term in the gardening textbooks. He brought such realism to his first broadcast that it sounded as though he was merely pausing on his spade as he spoke. And when Fred instructed his listeners to dig a two-foot trench, he didn't dismiss it as some triviality that would somehow dig itself. He knew it was darned hard work and he said so!

"Cooor," he warned, "I'll bet you'll know you've dug that blessed trench when you try to get out of bed next morning; but it's all in a good cause because the runner beans you'll be sowing there are real heavy feeders. So I want you to put plenty of compost into that trench, and all that lovely rich garden waste that's been maturing during the winter is just the stuff to get your runners off to a flying start! And for goodness sake, when you sow those beans, do give them plenty of space – nine inches to a foot apart. Some people think they can cram them in like the crowds in Piccadilly Circus. That's the biggest mistake they ever made in their lives!"

On that Sunday afternoon in 1935 Fred's rolling Sussex tones had put the country's loudspeakers to a pretty stern test. He had worked on the reasonable belief that folk all over Britain would be tuning in to hear him, and he hadn't the slightest intention of disappointing them. No wonder he was promptly classed as the loudest speaker to attack a microphone so far.

Later that day, back home at Petworth in Sussex, he was sternly reminded by his wife that he had scarcely sounded a single 'h' throughout the broadcast. Never mind. When the letters began to arrive next morning at Broadcasting House, they were rich in such phrases as 'a joy to listen to' and 'one of the few gardening broadcasts I've really been able to follow'. It wasn't until ten years later that Fred won his own regular spot on the air; but even as the Producer faced that first flood of letters, he knew that he had a valuable property in Fred – while Fred for his part awoke to the strange awareness that, at 58, he had just been launched on a new career. Yet how was it – why was it – that Fred had come to make that first improbable Sunday journey from the placid gardens of Petworth to Portland Place?

In the mid-1930's broadcasting moved at a leisurely pace. Carol Gibbons and the Savoy Hotel Orpheans held sway on the air most weekday tea-times. Still far in the future were all those breathless, eye-witness reports from distant battlegrounds – and the only really shocking news on the wireless was that Fred Perry had lost a set at Wimbledon. All the more surprising to find that something rather special was happening to the Nation's listening habits on Sunday afternoons. Once Sunday lunch was over and the last of the dishes had been washed and dried, families by the thousand would make for their sitting rooms and gather round their wireless sets. Being Sunday they could be sure that most of the programmes on the B.B.C.'s National and Regional programmes would be staid if not downright serious. But they also knew that a new personality was breaking away from the traditional stuffiness of Sunday broadcasting – a broadcaster named C. H. Middleton with a programme called 'In your Garden'.

As you might guess, Middleton's programmes dealt

strictly with earthy topics; but his listeners weren't merely dedicated gardeners. Many husbands who heartily loathed the weekend chore of digging those suburban patches would tune in each Sunday to C. H. Middleton, simply because he sounded the exact opposite of the conventional broadcaster. People listened to Middleton not merely for what he said but for what he represented – the first unaffected and down-to-earth broadcaster.

There were some strange ideas about the wireless in those days. Most listeners pictured a broadcasting studio as an impersonal chasm of a place peopled by elegant gentlemen in full evening dress and earnest engineers. Of course, these ideas weren't all that far off the mark. There had been a time, not long before, when Lord Reith (then General Manager of the B.B.C.) demanded black tie and dinner jacket from all his evening news-readers. But Mr. Middleton wasn't cast in this mould. He was a gardener with a splendidly unpolished voice who sought no hint of stardom but was hell bent on making the British better gardeners. So as his programme 'In your Garden' won more and more listeners he decided to widen his range of speakers by inviting other gardeners to join him at the microphone. And that was where Fred came in.

Fred and C. H. Middleton had been friends since well before the First World War, though it has to be said that, in those early days, their friendship came near to foundering on the rock of professional competition.

"It happened like this," Fred once explained to me. "I'd been exhibiting some rather special begonias at one of the R.H.S. Shows in London. Well Mr. Middleton (or 'Middy' as we gardeners always called him) was working for a very big nursery at the time and he managed to get hold of a few of my plants to build up a stock for himself." Fred smiled as he recounted the story, recalling how poor Mr. Middleton had been sorely perplexed by all this. "Well no sooner had he got those blessed begonias home Frank than he was

4

pulling them apart, trying to discover what I'd been feeding them on. As a matter of fact I'd been leaf-feeding them, so there was no hint of manure in the soil, and that had old Middy right worried. Anyhow he couldn't get them to root like I did and his firm was most upset about it. In fact, just a few weeks later he parted company with that particular nursery – and I always had the nasty feeling that my begonias had cost him his job."

"But surely Fred," I said, "You'd have to agree that Mr. Middleton was a first rate gardener in most respects."

"You want my honest opinion?" asked Fred. "You won't find many of us chaps who'll admit that another gardener knows what he's talking about. We're critical old buffers in the main, and that's how it was with Middy and me. Take the matter of digging. I remember reading a book that old Middy once wrote, full of all sorts of plans and diagrams showing you how to dig your garden. Never seen anything like it . . . made it more like a mathematical problem than plain gardening Frank! No, you've got to remember that this systematic digging business can be taken a lot too far. And that was only one case where Middy and I didn't see eye to eye."

In fact, the gardening philosophies of Fred and C. H. Middleton were often at odds, both on fundamental and on strictly trivial matters. For instance, Fred didn't like the way that Middy would label his seedboxes – too untidy and too haphazard by far, according to the meticulous Fred. His belief was that everything in the garden, the greenhouse and the potting shed should be labelled at every stage in its career; and he underlined his point by stressing the amount of time and plain bad temper that can be expended on the task of trying to identify a row of anonymous seedlings or a box of unmarked bulbs.

More fundamentally, the two men simply could not agree upon the point where Nature in the wild should be allowed to meet the cultured and cosseted world of our own gardens. Fred loved wild flowers and the sweet disorder of the woods and the hedgerows. In creating *his* gardens he was constantly trying to capture the spirit of Nature and to emulate the easy way she brings improbable plants and flowers together in perfect partnership. Some of the borders still to be seen at Petworth speak eloquently of the successes he had in creating the truly *natural* garden.

C. H. Middleton was a man of more formality in his gardens. Unlike Fred, he hated weeds. They had no place in his gardening scheme of things and once he wrote that 'General hygiene in the garden is of the utmost importance and this includes the ruthless destruction of weeds, particularly those allied to the vegetable crop.' Fred's reply to this was that some of the so-called weeds have a delicacy of flower and form that could teach many of the much vaunted blooms a lesson. Whether or not C. H. Middleton explored this controversial territory in any of his broadcasts, he certainly respected Fred's point of view. For early in 1935 he paid a visit to Petworth and asked Fred bluntly – "How about doing a broadcast with me? You've got the right sort of voice – and you've even got one or two good ideas. Why not join me up in London one day?"

"Not a hope," Fred replied. "I'd be as nervous as a kitten for one thing, and anyhow I'm far too busy gardening to get mixed up with your broadcasting larks."

Fred was a man not easily swayed. The plain truth was that the world of broadcasting held not the faintest interest or appeal for him – while the idea of stepping before a microphone to voice his opinions on gardening had never crossed his mind. Yet C. H. Middleton clearly had a persuasive tongue for at length it was arranged that, two Sundays later, Fred Streeter would journey to London to be a guest speaker on 'In your Garden'.

Fred was never one to take chances and, though the broadcast was scheduled for 2.15, his train from Sussex arrived in London at half-past-ten in the morning. He made at once for Broadcasting House.

This strange new building was something of a tourist attraction in those days. It reared up like a white Colossus at the foot of Portland Place, and those of us who have had the pain or privilege of making our first broadcasts from 'B.H.' will know that even today it does exert a strangely intimidating influence. Indeed if a first-time broadcaster dares to turn his thoughts to what lies in store for him, who could wonder if he turned on his heel and made an unseemly dash for freedom down Regent Street?

Fred looked up at Broadcasting House and wished devoutly he'd said 'No!' to Mr. Middleton. Remarkable, in a sense, that he'd managed to journey thus far. But now, looking up at that imposing white facade and down at the commissionaire who brooded over the doorway, Fred simply could not muster the courage to step inside.

High on Broadcasting House the clock moved relentlessly on while Fred took another fretful turn down Portland Place. Meanwhile, up in the rehearsal studio, the Producer was consulting his watch with increasing frequency. This gardener from Sussex might be a great horticulturist but he was certainly no timekeeper. As for Middy, he could not imagine why his supremely dependable friend, Fred Streeter, should choose this of all occasions to be late.

Was it perhaps that Mr. Streeter had somehow arrived unannounced? Down to the Hall went the Producer's secretary in an attempt to solve the mystery.

"No one of that name down here Miss," she was told in the flatly non-committal tones of an experienced commissionaire. Then he added: "But there *is* a little chap who keeps pacing up and down outside and sometimes peering through the windows. Don't suppose that could be him."

The secretary darted out into the street, spotted the footsore Fred and within seconds he was being pressed through the swing doors, shot into a lift, and carried at speed to the third floor. As the small, greying figure of Fred Streeter made its way through the studio doors, the production team noted with some surprise that the man about to dispense gardening wisdom to the nation was considerably older than the typical first-time broadcaster and yet carried himself with remarkable youthfulness.

For the first time in his life Fred now seated himself before a microphone – not, of course, one of those slim and silvery microphones of today but a circular instrument not unlike an enlarged telephone mouthpiece mounted on a firm, bronze-coloured base. His script was placed before him on a small wickerwork stand at precisely the right angle for easy reading; then Fred was introduced to the method of arranging his script, so that the risk of hearing papers making obtrusive rustling sounds over the air should be reduced to a minimum.

"Arrange your sheets rather like playing cards, Mr. Streeter," he was instructed. "Place them all in order of course, but with one sheet slightly overlapping the next. Then, when you've read to the bottom of one particular page, gently sweep it away with your hand. That will avoid the sound of papers being *turned*. Avoid turning the pages at all costs. These microphones are very sensitive to anything like that and to hear papers being turned rather spoils the sense of realism for listeners."

"Well Frank," said Fred, "There I was at the microphone with all those papers in front of me and the Producer saying 'Right Mr. Streeter ... we'll have a run through now shall we?' And away I went, reading from my script and doing my best to emphasise the points that needed emphasising and to chuckle when I thought I was being a bit funny. I took it fairly slowly mark you so as not to stumble over my words – and through a sort of glass panel affair I could see old 'Middy' watching me. He was even smiling now and again, so obviously he thought I was doing all right!"

Listening critically to Fred's first effort at the microphone, the Producer was inclined to agree with Mr. Middleton. Fred *had* done remarkably well in his rehearsal. There were only one or two phrases that sounded a shade stilted and needed revising – sentences that had the hallmark of the written word rather than the spoken word.

"Fine," said the Producer as Fred finished. "Fine indeed – now perhaps you could round off one or two of the corners where it's still a bit rough at the edges."

"Imagine that," said Fred, remembering the incident. "I looked at my script and the corners looked square enough to me. But old 'Middy' chipped in and sort of saved my life! 'All that's wanted Fred,' he explained, 'is for you to put those one or two sentences into a conversational form – the sort of language you'd use if you were chatting to me down in the garden at Petworth. Nothing wrong with most of it. Just make it sound more natural here and there.' "

Fred got the message . . . a message that served him well for the rest of his broadcasting career. For while he found it pleasantly reassuring to have a script in front of him throughout that first broadcast, he used it merely to keep himself on the right tracks, not as slavish word-by-word dicta.

Though peas and beans were the stars of the show in Fred's maiden programme, he also found time to spare a few words for potatoes – a crop which loves to be treated with kindness! He told his audience to work plenty of compost deep into the soil and to use their lawn mowings as an additional mulch. This would not only help the crop to develop but would ensure that the tubers came out clean and fresh without a hint of scab. And on the subject of digging the potatoes, it was his belief that they should be taken from the ground the very moment they were ready – since disease will often strike at potatoes that are over-mature and transform a first-rate crop into a disastrous yield. All this, and more, he told his listeners that memorable Sunday

9

afternoon!

"The strange thing was," Fred recalled, "that no sooner were we actually on the air and chatting away than a fellow in the studio was giving us the winding up signal and old 'Middy' was saying 'thank you and goodbye' to the listeners."

Yet for all its brevity, Fred had enjoyed his first broadcast. The Producer was full of smiles; 'Middy' was saying 'Well done Fred, you must join us again.' And the secretary was quietly tidying up the studio. As Fred made his way back to Petworth later that afternoon he pondered the thought that millions of people he would never meet in life had now heard his voice; and millions more might come to hear him in the days ahead, always supposing he was invited to broadcast again.

These were prophetic thoughts. Forty years later one author was to write of him – 'The best known voice in England since Winston Churchill's belongs to an elfin ninety-seven-year-old Sussex gardener with the unremarkable name of Fred Streeter.'

II

"If you're going to be a really good gardener you must *be adventurous. Don't stick to the same old shrubs and flowers year after year. Search through the catalogues. Discover what's new. Then if you come across a variety that does specially well in your garden, don't keep it all to yourself will you? Tell your neighbours. As likely as not their soil conditions will be the same as yours . . . so they can enjoy it too!"*

It takes a special kind of genius to find excitement in the pages of a seed catalogue. It takes a special kind of talent to coax a spirit of adventure from a vegetable patch. Fred Streeter had just such talent . . . just such genius. Gardening for him *was* an exciting business.

He had a particular interest in roses; and though he insisted that there were far too many varieties in the catalogues, he pioneered the idea of 'clothing' a bank or a flower bed with bush roses. This he did by running a series

11

of supporting wires about two feet over the bed and then training the shoots on to the wires. The stakes and the wires soon disappear beneath the foliage – and the results he once described to me as 'a magic carpet of roses'.

He was fascinated too by the growing of exotic fruits – not merely the relatively simple peaches and nectarines but the more ambitious pineapples and melons. With pineapples he developed his own favourite potting medium of fibrous loam, charcoal and broken brick – and he fervently preached the gospel that pineapples thrive best in a mainly dry environment; meanwhile with melons he frowned on those who are too generous with the watering can and the plant foods. Split melons – as Fred insisted – are a sorry sight; which is why he urged us to be on the frugal side when it comes to feeding the maturing plants.

Fred also voiced some highly controversial views on the matter of pruning. His basic belief was in rigorous pruning – and he had no time at all for the gardener who merely snips indecisively with his secateurs. Vigorous pruning, he maintained, presents a new and growing challenge to a plant. 'If you go for a haircut Frank,' he would say, 'you know full well that your hair will get a new lease of life. Yet the way some gardeners go on, you'd imagine that hard pruning was more or less a death sentence for the poor old plant!'

Never mind that some gardeners didn't always see eye to eye with him. Fred's firm convictions lent a lively spirit of controversy and adventure to his work; and it showed not only in his gardening but in his broadcasting too. 'Gardens thrive on change just like the rest of us,' he would insist. 'Take the vegetable garden for instance. You'd *expect* to find sprouts and cabbages and lettuces there wouldn't you? But why leave it at that? How about trying a row of endive as well? It's got a slightly bitter flavour that's the making of a salad! And how many gardeners do you know who've ever tried growing aubergine? Not many I'll bet. They're scared somehow. They're just not adventurous enough.'

Fred had a theory that any vegetable with a continental sounding name stood only a slender chance of being planted in the typical British back garden. But those who caught his infectious spirit of adventure soon discovered that it really did pay dividends. They would write expansive letters to him, telling of the new world of horticulture he had introduced to them; and, thus inspired, they would vow to blaze new trails from the seclusion of the vegetable patch. One correspondent even sent thanks to Fred for introducing him to the Globe Artichoke; he had read in several gardening books that this is not a suitable vegetable for the small plot; but then he had heard Fred say that it was a majestic plant with a splendidly delicate flavour to reward the gardener – so he had tried growing the Globe Artichoke for himself. Unfortunately he had allowed one or two of his plants to flower, with the result that instead of finding the artichokes had a soft and fleshy centre (as well as those succulent 'petals'), they had turned strangely fibrous and unpleasant to the palate.

"Never let the globe artichoke flower", Fred replied to the letter writer. "Always eat them well before the first flowers appear – then they'll be delicious with a vinegar dressing or even just a knob of butter and salt. But I'm so pleased you're getting a bit more adventurous in your gardening."

For Fred's own part, the first hint of adventure had come into his life long before he knew of the earthy career that lay ahead of him; and his first contact with the soil had come perilously close to being his last.

At the age of two, Fred was already a child with an eye for the garden. He had clambered uncertainly on to the window ledge of his bedroom to take a peep at the trim cottage garden below, using the canvas window blinds as a sheet anchor. The blinds looked firm enough; just fine for a fingerhold. And so they proved to be, until he taxed their

13

endurance a little too far. The blinds ripped and Fred shot head first out of the window, straight into his father's bed of pinks below.

"I don't mind telling you," Fred recalled, "my Dad wasn't all that pleased. But once he'd made sure his pinks were all right he took me indoors to make sure *I'd* come to no harm. There were no bones broken – and no blooms damaged. So the whole affair was soon forgotten."

The infant Fred got little sympathy despite the fact that he was a far from robust baby. Yet, from that day on, his health steadily began to improve – nurtured by the good clean air that blew straight from the South Downs across the fields and gardens of the Sussex village of Pulborough where the Streeter family had their home.

Both his parents came from worthy Sussex stock, and though Fred had only fleeting recollections of his grandparents he knew for certain that their roots too had been in this county of gentle pasturelands and rolling hills.

"As a child," said Fred, "I wasn't encouraged to ask too many questions. Those were the days when children were meant to be seen and not heard. But I *do* remember my mother telling me that she herself had been a post-girl. Jolly hard work it was too, tramping round all those farms where she had to deliver the letters – and all for half-a-crown a week."

Hard times no doubt. Yet even during his early schooldays in Pulborough Fred Streeter was developing a sensitive nose and an appreciative palate for some of the finer things of life. Bread coming hot from the village baker's oven on a crisp winter's morning. The heavy scent of lavender growing high above the cottage garden wall. The Sussex orchards where the cider apples grew and where the tasting of the first brew really did separate the men from the boys.

'Pigeon's Gate' was the name of the cottage where Fred made that spectacular fall into the pinks. It stood on the borders of the farm where his father, James Streeter, worked as a shepherd. James was not a disciplinarian in the true Victorian tradition. But he was a staunch patriot, which perhaps explains why one of Fred's earliest memories finds him standing in the main street of Pulborough fervently waving a paper Union Jack as a parade of soldiers marches by. The date was 1887, Queen Victoria's Jubilee Year; and though the elderly Queen was a remote figure in his mind, the mere fact that she had reigned for fifty Glorious Years sent a surge of patriotism through his veins.

Right through life he retained his enthusiasm. He practised the maxim that you can't expect anyone to become keen on the soil and all it has to offer unless you sound enthusiastic too. And at the age of five it was just such keenness that eventually won the day when he pleaded with his father to be given his own little plot of land to cultivate in the Streeter's cottage garden at Pulborough.

Roses and radishes were the improbable partners of his first garden and he poured a lot of thought, a lot of love into tending them. But all too soon — before the fruits of his labours could be enjoyed — he had to part with his garden. His father had found a better job, tending a special herd of Shorthorn cattle across the county border in Surrey. And here, near Dorking, Fred Streeter was soon happily settled at North Holmwood School.

"Strange how quickly you can adapt to change when you're young," said Fred. "And it seems to me, looking back, that I'd forgotten about Pulborough in a month or two . . . almost as if I'd never lived there. But I loved that little school at North Holmwood — and school work was everything now."

Three years in succession he gained the school medal for punctual attendance; and though the Headmaster was quick to recognise the bookish skills of this particular pupil, he also discovered from brief discussions with Fred that his first and absorbing interest was in gardening.

"There was a *real* headmaster for you and no mistake. Couldn't stand untidiness; everything had to be just so," Fred recalled. "To make matters worse, the school pathways and flower borders were getting all overgrown with weeds. So was the little vegetable plot. Proper mess they were, because the regular chap had left you see."

The headmaster saw that Fred could put matters right and decided that he was to spend half an hour each week tending those gardens; though, as Fred conceded, "What he thought I could do in thirty minutes I really can't imagine!"

Fred never claimed to be a particularly fast worker. But he *was* a born planner. He would look at a job in the garden, reduce it to its simplest terms, then tackle it with his predetermined plan – an approach that certainly owed something to those days of basic gardening at North Holmwood.

With a new garden, for instance, his method was to draw up an outline sketch and then to divide the area into four parts, allotting a specific role to each of those squares. Into the first square would go the permanent crops like the fruit trees, the herb garden, the redcurrant and blackcurrant bushes. Next came the square for plants with a hearty appetite – potatoes and onions for instance; this was therefore the plot on which to lavish most of the lawn clippings and leaf mould. The third square was reserved for fast-maturing crops – the salad stuff such as lettuce and radishes and the fast-growing spinach. Finally, the fourth square was for root crops – and this was the area where plenty of digging paid dividends. Many a gardener asks himself sadly why his carrots and parsnips are such shapeless disasters. The reason, often enough, is simply that they have encountered all manner of obstacles on their tortuous journey into the soil!

Even in those early days at North Holmwood, Fred's methodical mind was serving him well, and he worked miracles with the school garden. No wonder that when the time arrived to move to another school in nearby Reigate, he took with him a note written in glowing terms – confirming that here was a pupil who had a winning way with anything to do with the soil.

"Fine . . . fine," muttered Fred's new head teacher, casting an approving eye over the letter and smiling benevolently at his pupil. "You like gardening I see. But what do you like *in particular*?"

"Flowers sir," Fred answered promptly, hoping that here was his passport to horticultural promotion.

"Good, good," replied the Head, "then in future you will be responsible for cleaning out the greenhouses!"

"Probably did me good Frank," he confided. "Stopped me getting too big for my boots. Because around that time one of the other masters was telling me I was jolly good at essay writing. He even got me to enter an essay competition where we had to write about 'Alcohol and the Human Body'. Cooor . . . what a caper that was!"

In fact, Fred won first prize in that competition. But so deep (and so revealing) had been his research into the subject of alcohol and its attendant horrors that he resolved never to become a 'drinking man' himself. Other children might cadge a drop of cider from the farm workers; other boys might boast of illicit sips of beer – but not Fred.

It would be all too easy to class Fred Streeter as a typical, puritanical product of the mid-Victorian era. This was partly true. Yet he had a ready turn of wit which was by no means always prudish; and his laughter at a well told joke was itself a joy to hear. Nevertheless, Fred the schoolboy was an earnest, unsmiling student. He took his lessons seriously and was earmarked in the classification of those days as 'a lad with prospects'.

Those words were amply justified when the time arrived to think of wider academic horizons, for he took the

17

entrance exam for Reigate Grammar School and had no difficulty passing. But the simple truth was that he did not want to go there. The school had very definite ideas about the type of careers to which its pupils should aspire. The learned professions, for instance, and vocations such as Medicine. But *gardening*? No boy on record had ever entered the school with the improbable aim of becoming a gardener. It was this conflict of interests that found a far from contrite Streeter making his way to the Headmaster's study, there to discuss the world of opportunity that lay ahead.

Doctor Fox was the Headmaster's name. Plain speaking was one of his many virtues. He told Fred bluntly to forget about being a gardener. He should turn his thoughts to becoming a teacher instead. And if for some obscure reason teaching didn't quite appeal to him – why then, there were plenty of office jobs that would pay far better than gardening. "You'll never make money as a gardener. Forget it. With your brain you deserve a far better future than that."

Eighty years after that meeting, Fred sat with me in his little dining room at Petworth and chuckled at the memory. Then he pulled out the linings of his trouser pockets to reveal their blameless emptiness.

"See Frank. The old doctor was right. You never make much money as a gardener. But if I had my time all over again – I'd do just the same. And do you know . . . less than a week after that visit to the Headmaster's study, I was earning a living as a gardener's lad. If you could call it a living!"

Fred was employed as the 'new boy' at Colley Lodge – a sizeable house on Reigate Heath with gardens that had a reputation for their year-round variety and unfailing neatness. His pay was half-a-crown for a six day week, twelve hours a day. Reveille was at 6 a.m. when he made the rounds of the greenhouses, recording the temperatures; then came the task of flower-pot washing until breakfast time. But it was *after* breakfast that the problems of the day really began.

There were no mechanical cultivators in those days. No motor mowers. So the new boy's job was to lead the overweight pony who pulled the lawn mower over the rolling acres of velvet-smooth grass, and though this may sound a reasonably simple task, it had its pitfalls.

The head gardener of this Surrey estate took particular pride in his lawn edges – "Crisp and sharp is the way I like them – and crisp and sharp is the way we'll have them!"

"Bit of an old blighter he was, to tell the truth," said Fred. "This was his first place as Head Gardener – and didn't we all know it! There was only one of us who wasn't scared of him . . . and that was the old pony!"

The pony did not like the Head Gardener. Still less did he like the task of pulling the lawn mower. He therefore formed the habit of quietly steering the lawn mower away from the smoothness of the lawns and over the immaculate edges. This caused the machine to bump and lurch which, to the pony's mind, made an interesting diversion during the long working day. But the manoeuvre also caused some bizarre contours to appear on those well kept edges, and Fred soon came to realise that a Head Gardener's wrath can be mighty indeed.

"Seems to me," Fred recalled, "That never a day went by when I was a gardener's boy without *something* happening that would stick in my memory . . . like the time I helped to bury a poor old bullock at Colley Lodge!"

There are probably few gardeners alive today who can remember the ritual burial of farm animals. According to Fred, the entire garden staff would be mustered for these sombre occasions, not merely to provide a labour force for digging a suitable hole but also to stand in reverence by the grave as the animal was laid to rest.

"The idea," Fred explained, "was that the creature's skeleton would gradually decompose to provide the soil with a wonderful supply of bonemeal. So the bullock we buried at Colley Lodge was dug in nice and close to one of the vineries – and as the ceremony got under way, all of us lads were meant to offer up a prayer that the poor old animal would be just as useful in death as we hoped he'd been in life. The only trouble was that I couldn't help thinking that whatever had killed the bull in the first place might kill off the vines as well . . . though of course I didn't admit such wicked thoughts to the Head Gardener."

Another memorable milestone in those early days was Fred's introduction to his first really sizeable tree. This was the ornamental pine tree with the weighty name, *Pinus Ponderosa*; and Fred recalled how his love of woodland settings dated from the day he raised his eyes to the eighty foot heights of that wonderful pine tree in the gardens of Colley Lodge.

Despite these moments of contemplation, most of his duties were still sternly earthbound, though he was the first to agree that even the chore of keeping the greenhouse brasswork highly polished had its own salutary lesson to teach him.

"No doubt about it," said Fred, "if that brasswork wasn't glowing bright, then we boys were in real trouble. You had to be able to see your face in those door handles – and it was the same with the roses of the watering can; but I've got to admit that it paid off in later years. In fact, I took special pride in having the cleanest can in the garden . . . and woe betide any lad who tried to swop his can for mine. I looked after that can just as if it were a five-pound note – and to this very day I can't stand seeing a mucky can or a trowel all caked with soil. Give everything a quick polish before you put it in the shed – because good housekeeping is just as important in the garden as it is indoors, even if that does sound Double Dutch!"

"Another thing about those early days Frank; we used to fumigate the greenhouses by letting shreds of tobacco smoulder there. I suppose it worked after a fashion because it was pretty rough old shag we used, though I don't imagine the scientists would approve of the method these days. Anyhow, it was my job to stay in the greenhouse while all this fumigation was going on, just to make sure that the place didn't catch fire. It was a rotten old job, I can tell you, and I'd often find myself spluttering and choking fit to drop. But at least it cured me of ever wanting to smoke. So there I was, still in my teens, but already a non-smoker and a non-drinker. In fact it seemed to some of the lads that I was a bit of a goody-goody and they began to pull my leg about it!"

Yet although young Fred made few friends among his colleagues in the 'bothy', (the outhouse where the apprentices made their home), another more enduring friendship was now being cemented. He loved the flowers he cared for just as if they were human. He credited them with powers of reasoning and perception. Their life, he believed, was a blend of pain and pleasure just like ours, and he spoke with firm conviction of 'the melody of the flowers'. He gloried in the paradise of new blossoms that greeted the changing seasons of the year; and even the tall and swaying grasses of the Surrey fields seemed to him to have a lesson to teach us all.

"Stand in a field of long grass Frank," he would advise, "and listen to those grasses talking. They don't fall out with the grasses in the next field do they? Not likely. But we humans . . . talk about touchy. Never satisfied unless we're having an argument with someone."

Years earlier, back in the bothy after a long day's work in the gardens, young Fred had sometimes tried a little of this homespun philosophy on one or two of the more thoughtful apprentices. Most of it fell on unreceptive, even unbelieving ears.

How could flowers have feelings? How could grasses talk? The other boys in the bothy saw their daily lot in a very different light. There were flower pots to be scoured, brasses to be polished, greenhouse floors to be scrubbed, borders to weed, edges to clip. And when *that* little round of duties was safely completed, the Head Gardener would be waiting with his slate at the ready, all set to recite another uninspiring list of tasks. If you could cope with all that and still find time to listen to the melody of the flowers and the whisperings of the grasses, you weren't just conscientious. You were dedicated!

"I stuck to that job at Reigate Heath for about three years," Fred admitted. "Then I said to myself 'Freddy my boy, it's time for a change'." And after a brief spell in a Reigate nursery, he had his first taste of private service in the gardens of a really 'Big House'.

That house was Reigate Priory. The owner was Lady Henry Somerset. And when Fred arrived the gardens were undergoing an exciting period of change. New greenhouses were going up. New flower borders and shrubberies were being established. There was even a newly built tree house at the Priory and young Fred would watch with awe as Lady Somerset swept through the gardens and up the spiral staircase, finally to disappear within the tree-house where she would quietly pen a letter or two in true communion with Nature.

Those gardens possessed a magical fragrance that Fred could always recapture: a blend of honeysuckle and lavender, of camomile and columbine, each making its own bid for favour. They endeared themselves to the young apprentice and gave him renewed assurance that he had chosen the right job in life.

His confidence was strengthened still further when he was promoted to the care of a group of special hot-houses, including a peach house and a fig house. Already he was moving into that world of semi-exotic fruits which were to hold such fascination for him in later life. Yet few of his contemporaries who were to admire his talents in the growing and the judging of fruits ever realised that, to use his own words, he personally "couldn't stand the stuff".

Seldom would you see any sort of fruit on Fred Streeter's table. Never raw; rarely cooked. And this strange aversion to fruit dated back to a bitter experience in the fig house at Reigate when he dared to ask the foreman gardener if he might sample one of the developing fruit.

"Course you can boy," said his boss with a smile. "Try this one!" And he tossed Fred a large but totally unripe fig.

Fred couldn't – or wouldn't – admit that he hated it. There was a barrier of formality between apprentice and foreman that allowed of no such concessions, and somehow he forced himself to swallow the lot.

"Talk about *sour*," said Fred, shutting his eyes in remembered horror. "I'll never forget that fig till the day I die. Even then it'll likely haunt me!"

But if that was a bitter memory, bitter in another sense were some of the fruit pruning duties this very same foreman was to delegate to Fred during his early days at the Priory.

"He was a great one for his winter pruning," Fred admitted, "but he was a chap who never seemed to feel the cold. Early in December he'd have us out in the orchard, reminding us that all the pruning had to be finished pretty quickly before we started spraying with the winter wash. But it's my belief that the gardener should try and *avoid* pruning on those really bitter days. He'll never make a good job of it if he feels that his fingers are about to drop off. No . . . you wait for one of the milder days we usually get in December; and provided you've got a really sharp knife and a good quality pair of secateurs, you can polish off your pruning before you know you've started!"

Despite the stern treatment he received at the hands of the foreman, this was a time when exciting new horizons were beginning to open for Fred – opportunities that brought precisely the note of challenge he felt was lacking

23

in his life. Lady Henry Somerset owned not only Reigate Priory but also a splendid town house in Park Lane; and the more floral colour she could see in her London home, the better she was pleased. It pleased her too that a gardener as young as Fred should display such a tutored eye for beauty; so she decided that he should be her courier on a series of missions from Surrey to London.

Most of the flowers that were needed for the Town House Fred would take from the Reigate gardens; but to achieve a really wide-ranging selection, he would buy still more in Covent Garden. And though, in the early days, he would be accompanied on these missions by one of the more senior gardeners, it was soon clear that he had a natural talent for selecting the right flowers for the occasion – and for arranging them not merely with imagination but with a touch of inspiration too.

Those were the days, too, when window boxes were enjoying especial popularity and it was Fred's proud claim that, right through the year, the well tended window box can present a splendid splash of colour to brighten the drabbest day in the greyest of cities.

"Not that Lady Somerset's place in Park Lane was drab," he assured me, "not a bit of it. My floral decorations took care of that – and when she thought I'd put on a specially good display, she'd think up some little treat to reward me."

On one occasion she even gave him a theatre ticket for a first night at Her Majesty's Theatre in the Haymarket, where *The Seats of the Mighty* was being presented and the lead was taken by the legendary Beerbohm Tree.

"It was wonderful Frank . . . a lovely evening for me. The first time I'd been to a *real* theatre. But no sooner had I finished clapping when it was all over than I was in for a bit of a shock. I looked up at the clock and discovered it was close on midnight! Coor, that did it! The last train for Reigate was just about leaving Victoria."

No wonder that this particular first night lingered for ever in Fred's memory, not so much for *The Seats of the Mighty* as for the mighty long journey that lay ahead of him! When he left the theatre he pondered the possibility of a brisk walk to Park Lane to enquire whether a bed might be found for him 'below stairs'. But he dismissed this idea as altogether too presumptuous, apart from which he would be late for his gardening duties next morning.

The one remaining option was the twenty-mile tramp back to the Priory. The night was fine. The journey in those pre-motor car days held no real hazards; and the steady plod of his feet never faltered. But no sooner was he back in Reigate than the sun was rising and another day's work was about to begin.

"When the old Head Gardener asked me how I'd enjoyed the theatre," said Fred, "I just replied 'Very nice Sir' and left it at that! To tell you the truth, I was too whacked to say much more."

The next time Fred went to the theatre, he did not wait for the curtain calls. Instead he was out of his seat and heading for home with all speed – reasoning that if High Society could stay up to all hours, honest gardeners most certainly could not.

"I don't want to sound a miserable old buffer", Fred once admitted to me, "but a good gardener must have a bit of discipline in his life – and he's *got* to stick to a timetable just like the fruit and the flowers and the vegetables do. You wouldn't think much of daffodils that refused to bloom in the spring or tomatoes that couldn't be bothered to ripen in the summer. Same goes with the old gardener himself. If he's going to get good results, he's got to be pretty strict with his plants ... and he's got to set them a good example!"

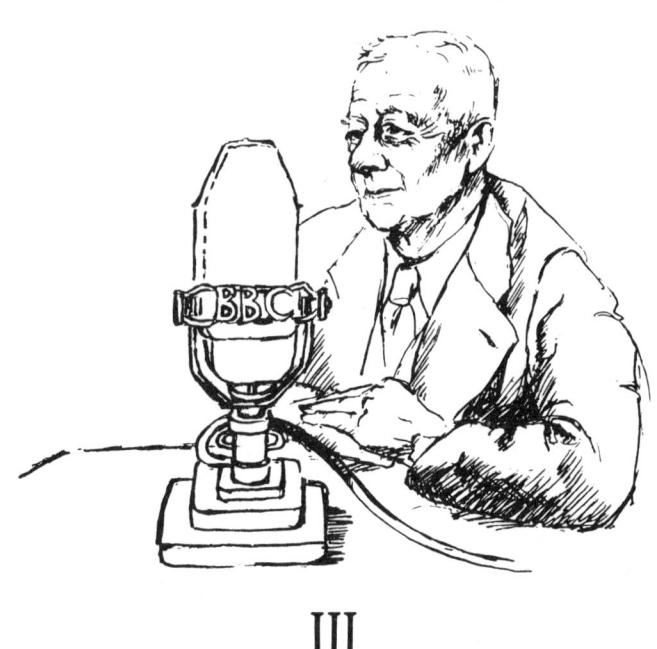

III

"Soak them thoroughly when you plant them out. Really drench the roots before you settle them into the soil. But after that don't give them another drop of water as long as they live. . . ."

This was Fred's advice on the way to treat outdoor tomatoes – another expression of his belief that a strict code of discipline must apply to the garden and the gardener alike. And as we sat in the rose-scented peace of the sunken gardens at Petworth recording those words, something told me that these were the most controversial lines he had ever spoken in the course of his broadcasting career.

Over the years he had carefully nurtured the belief among listeners that they should treat their trees and shrubs and flowers – even their vegetables too – very much like friends of the family. Yet here he was suggesting, with all the persuasion of those rolling Sussex tones, that we should callously ignore the raging thirst of our tomatoes –

even if they wilted in the summer heat and turned their drooping leaves towards us in a silent plea for water!

"Some folk are altogether too soft with their tomatoes," he insisted. "The moment they look that little bit thirsty, away they dash for the watering can – and they usually end up doing far more harm than good. No, you let them go thirsty!"

Fred's reasoning for his harshness towards our Money-makers and Market Kings was convincing enough. "If it rains," he explained, "that's Nature's way of giving the whole garden a good soaking and your tomatoes will say 'thanks very much'."

I nodded and waited to learn why the rains of Heaven were so much better than the humble bounty of the watering can.

"But when you take that little watering can to your tomatoes Frank, just think what you're doing. You're simply wetting a small patch of soil around the tomatoes and the poor young roots get all confused. *They* think it's raining and away they go, reaching out for more and more moisture – instead of which they soon find they're probing into dry territory and they've wasted all that energy for nothing!"

The way Fred stated the case it seemed proved beyond doubt. But as the letters poured in suggesting that on this occasion even the infallible Fred Streeter had gone a shade too far, the Great Tomato Controversy suddenly assumed a more personal flavour.

One lady listener threatened to visit Fred Streeter at Petworth, bringing with her not only some bottled tomatoes from last year's bumper (and well watered) crop, but also bringing several other ladies who were still in a state of shock over Fred's advice on the way to treat tomatoes. Happily the visit did not materialise for she sounded a formidable lady, intent on an ugly confrontation.

Another correspondent turned to Nature as his ally in

the battle he intended to wage against Fred Streeter. 'We are all the products of God', he wrote, 'and as God's most favoured creatures we have been given the power to help Nature when some of her lesser creatures are fighting for survival. So how can Fred Streeter deny us the right to bring succour to an ailing tomato plant?'

It was all very emotional stuff, and though I did my best to stand on the sidelines of the growing controversy, it wasn't long before I was not only involved but was labelled as one of Fred's staunch supporters in the anti-watering lobby.

The supposedly staid resort of Worthing on the Sussex Coast is my home town and also a great place for tomatoes. The amateur gardeners of Worthing knew full well that I was the other half of the Fred-and-Frank partnership and they would approach me in the street asking whether Fred had retracted at least part of his unequivocal advice. They would corner me in shops, hoping to take the discussion a stage further and inviting me to pay a visit to their young but already prospering tomato plants. The saucier elements among the townsfolk would wink at me as we passed on the pavement and enquire – "Grown any good tomatoes lately?"

To all such critics I had the ready-made response: "I'm only the chap who asks the questions. It's Fred who gives the answers."

As the Great Tomato Controversy raged on, Fred was neither surprised nor even mildly penitent. He knew from past experience that tomato culture can prove a strangely touchy subject. But he was sorry that I should be saddled with the task of explaining his theory time and time again, and very soon he came up with a simple way for me to put the critics to flight.

"Ask them," he advised with a chuckle, "whether they're interested in growing plenty of tomatoes . . . or plenty of tomato leaves. If they're keen on the leaves, tell

28

them to give their plants all the water they can take. Nothing like water for growing lovely foliage!"

The stark simplicity of the message was my salvation. No gardener can doubt that plenty of leaves and plenty of moisture go hand in hand. Yet even to this day the Nation remains fiercely divided on the issue and there are many gardeners who still reach for the hose or the watering can the moment a hint of yellow appears on a single tomato leaf.

Speaking one summer's afternoon to a Women's Institute Meeting at Goring in Sussex, I was faced by a middle-aged lady who had clearly lost faith in Fred Streeter. She had only half heard his 'no watering' advice and had promptly applied it to her *greenhouse* tomatoes too. The results were swift and deadly. But while acknowledging that she herself had blundered, she still maintained in ringing tones that "Mr. Streeter can't be *quite* as kindly a gentleman as I always thought he was!"

Fred Streeter *was* kind — a very kind man. He was thoughtful to those who worked for him over the years; he was considerate to those who sought his advice. Most important of all, he lavished unstinting love on the gardens he tended, and I went to some lengths to tell this lady so. But there is a wealth of difference between kindness and softness; and years earlier, when the young Fred Streeter had first decided that gardening was to be the career for him, he also resolved to prepare himself physically for the taxing times that lay ahead.

"I always remember a little verse," he said, "that you'll still see displayed in many a country garden Frank. It goes something like this —

> Adam was a gardener
> And God who made him sees
> That half a *proper* gardener's work
> Is done upon his knees!"

29

Fred took the message to heart. Like Adam, he meant to be a proper gardener — and if this meant taxing his body well beyond its normal limits, then he was prepared to do just that.

Even in his very young days Fred had proved himself to be a powerful walker. Long tramps over the Surrey hills had prepared his leg muscles for the assaults that lay ahead. But while still at Reigate he decided to take up walking as a serious sport; and since the calls of duty were taking him more and more to London, he hit on the idea of applying for membership of the Polytechnic Harriers.

The Harriers could field a formidable team of walkers and admission to their ranks was strictly on merit. When Fred mentioned to them some of his successes at the local Reigate Sports they were sympathetically interested but not especially impressed; but when he told them that in the Army's Open Sports at Aldershot he had returned a time of six minutes thirty-three seconds for the grass mile, there was a prompt welcome for him providing he could manage to combine the demands of gardening with the many calls to training sessions.

Fred therefore set himself a stringent routine which taught him a lesson that he often repeated to me: "If you're really keen on something, really interested, you haven't got time or inclination to keep looking at the clock and asking yourself whether it's time to knock off. After all . . . watching the time is the biggest time waster of all!"

Certainly no time was wasted in the days Fred spent at Reigate Priory. On a typical evening in Spring he could well be busy sowing in the vegetable garden or working in one of the shrubberies until the last rays of daylight faded. But then — while his colleagues would take a quick cold-water wash in the bothy and cycle off into Reigate to meet their lady friends — Fred would slip into his dark blue vest and knee-length shorts and stride into the country lanes, with only the rhythmic crunch of his feet on gravel to keep him company.

These were golden days at Reigate Priory until – for a most unlikely reason – a note of discord was sounded. Fred was always an early riser, insisting that in the first moments of every dawn (when the day itself is still uncertain about the delights or disasters it has in store for us) the gardener has his own best moments for reviewing the success of yesterday's toils and the hopes and aspirations for today's.

Sad to say the original Head Gardener at Reigate Priory had now moved on, to be replaced by a stern unsmiling man from Yorkshire; and while the new man had a high regard for his own achievements in the world of horticulture (and a stack of prize certificates to confirm his talent) he had no time at all for Fred Streeter's early rising habits.

Morning after morning he was awakened by the crunch of a wheelbarrow and a gaily whistled tune beneath his bedroom window; and while a couple of warnings to Fred brought a temporary respite, soon it was clear that the vital bond of compatibility did not – and could never – exist between the man from Yorkshire and the eager aspirant from Sussex. It was time for Fred to move on, but not without certain regrets and a host of memories.

Fred kept a detailed diary in those days. He believed that every gardener should do so, not only to supplement the more formal records that must be maintained in every sizeable garden but to note the more personal aspects of success and failure. Fred's diary told its own little story of progress; how he had been promoted to take charge of two vineries, a grading house and two peach houses – and how he had helped to establish at Reigate Priory a particularly fine collection of bay trees. The flower gardens had also prospered during his stay at the Priory; and though the new Head Gardener would certainly never concede that a young and untried assistant such as Fred could have helped to shape

31

the very character of those gardens, Fred knew in his heart that he had stamped something of his own personality upon them. The diary also made reference to some of the staff at Reigate Priory and made special mention of the Head Chef who ruled the kitchens there.

This strange, almost sinister, character had a penchant for birds, alive and dead. He kept pet jackdaws in the kitchen. And although with the help of strategically placed scraps of food he would encourage wilder birds into the kitchen too, he was not beyond slaying them with a wickedly sharp knife and – rumour had it – would sometimes even cook and eat his luckless victims. Also recorded in Fred's diary was the chef's Chinese recipe for making a model castle in rice, though it has to be said that the ingredients were not easy to come by. Around the castle battlements he would hang a necklace of real sparrows' skulls, as many as two hundred skulls to a single castle. Further decoration was provided by a selection of rare and colourful egg shells.

Saying goodbye to Reigate Priory wasn't merely a matter of a perfunctory handshake with the Yorkshire Head Gardener, a leave-taking nod to the chef and a warmer farewell to the more junior members of the staff; there was also the final glimpse of the gardens themselves and about this Fred had some sound advice to offer.

"When you're leaving a garden that you've carefully tended through all the changing seasons, don't feel ashamed Frank if you've a bit of a lump in your throat. It's only natural. After all, you are saying farewell to a good old friend. But here's what to do. Take a careful look around your garden before you go; see what little triumphs you've had – and what shocking mistakes you've made. This way you'll be taking a useful bit of experience with you. Of course, if you're moving to another garden of your own there's no reason why you shouldn't take a few cuttings along to remind you a bit of the past. But once you've closed the gate behind you, I shouldn't look back if I were you. Better to think of the future now. It's like life itself you know. No use dwelling too much on days gone by. It's tomorrow that really matters."

The 'tomorrow' that really mattered for Fred Streeter as he made his way from Reigate Priory was December 27th 1897. For this was the day he was due to report to James Veitch & Sons of Kings Road, Chelsea – a nursery whose reputation near the turn of the century was known and respected around the world.

Competition was fierce among aspiring young gardeners to be granted a spell of training at this Mecca of the horticultural world; and if discipline was strict, at least it carried the reward of saying to some future employer – 'Of course, sir, I've served my time with Veitch's of London.'

Today, perhaps, it is strange to think that a nursery of world-wide fame could have its growing headquarters in the heart of London. In those closing years of the nineteenth century, it seemed the most rational thing in the world. Veitch's were renowned not only for the variety of plants and flowers they could offer but for the breathtaking rarity of many of them. They had a reputation for bringing the exotic plants of the East to this country and for introducing the British gardener to the horticultural treasures of distant lands like South Africa and Siberia. Where better than London to display their triumphs?

For young Fred Streeter the early days of every new job seemed destined to be a time of high adventure. His introduction to Veitch's Nurseries was no exception.

Over the Christmas of 1897 London had been cloaked in a pea-soup fog which left its grimy hand-prints all over the capital. Fred was ordered to connect up a hose and to spray the glasshouses from end to end to remove all trace of this unwholesome silt. But the jet of water shot with such force from the hose-pipe that it missed the glasshouses completely and instead scored a direct hit on the top-hat of one of the firm's directors who happened to be passing at the time.

"What a frightful moment that was," Fred recalled. "And me the nervous new boy! But the old chap never said a word. He just rescued his hat, shook off the water, then away he went on his rounds."

Life in London for Fred was a strange amalgam of excitement at what lay ahead and regrets for those rural days at Reigate. In the evenings as he walked back to his Chelsea lodging house, through streets whose gardens were no more than postage-stamp patches of weary soil, he would recall those other evenings when he had walked the country lanes near Reigate.

After Sussex with its sweeping Downs and distant glimpses of the glittering sea those Surrey lanes had once seemed strangely restricting to Fred. How splendidly spacious they all seemed now. He even recalled with a warm nostalgia the many times he had turned out as a member of the Reigate Priory Cricket Team – a team which included amongst its fixtures an annual match against the Surrey County Eleven.

There had been one memorable game against a side which numbered the great W. G. Grace in its ranks; and Fred would relive that bitter-sweet moment when, with a monumental stroke, Grace had lofted a ball high into the sky and Fred had raced round the boundary with the glorious prospect of catching the great man out.

"They'd put me at the back of the bowler's arm," Fred explained, "and old W. G. Grace hit a ball that went right up in the air and someone in the crowd shouted 'Watch him boy . . . watch him boy . . . catch him!' Well I looked round to see who was talking – and the next thing I knew the ball had met me right on the chest and I was in among the spectators. Old W. G. ran over to me and said – 'That'll teach you to keep your eye on the ball lad!', then back he went to the wicket."

So instead of holding the catch of a lifetime, young Fred

came near to being felled by the Master; but when I asked him whether Grace had eventually spared him a word of sympathy, there was a cold finality to the answer.

"No . . . not a word," said Fred. "He never even said goodbye."

Despite harsh moments like this, Fred Streeter could still feel a wave of regret for those Reigate days as he turned into the gate of his humble Chelsea lodging house. How cosy that life in the Reigate bothy seemed now. How delicious the meals that he and the other boys had prepared – after a day which, for all its labours, had owed so much to the gentle softness of that Surrey garden.

Everything in London seemed so harsh. The clattering trams. The strident Cockney voices. The endless pavements. Most of all, the strange moods and manners of those who were now his room-mates.

In London he was now sleeping in a room with as many as sixteen others; and to supplement his wages he was sometimes working deep into the night, filling little packets with seeds or potting up plants in readiness for some glittering theatrical 'First Night'.

Despite those pavements, walking was still the favourite pursuit of his leisure hours; but now a new and absorbing interest had also entered his working life. Fred's foreman had enlisted his help in preparing the caladiums for the Temple Show – the fore-runner of today's Chelsea Flower Show. And to be entrusted with Veitch's caladiums had all the status – and all the responsibilities – of taking charge of the infant heir to the throne in a Royal household.

With the confidence of the man who has trodden this path many times before, the foreman explained to Fred the particular loves and hates of the caladium – or 'ornamental aroid' as the heavier gardening books will have it. The caladium demands complete rest in the winter and the tubers should be kept dry in the pots until March; then their interest in life reawakens.

35

In damp moss or peat and an encouraging temperature of about seventy degrees Fahrenheit (twenty-one degrees Centigrade) they will start to grow again until they are ready for planting into individual pots. This potting was to be Fred's responsibility and he was warned never to use a cracked pot but always to cover the crocks at the bottom of the pot with a little moss. This was to form a gentle barrier between soil and crocks so that efficient drainage should never be interrupted.

Advice like this wasn't. merely filed away in Fred's memory. It was noted in his diary too. And as the day for the opening of the Temple Show approached and the caladiums came near to their moment of perfection, Fred sensed the excitement he was to know so many times in years to come. The excitement, the hopes, the dreads and – who knows – the triumphs of the Big Show.

Such names they had, those caladiums that were now transferred to splendid tubs for display in the marquees of the Temple Show! *Caladium Chantinii* with its dramatic colouring of green, red and white. *Caladium Picturatum Adamantinum* with its white spotted veins and pink and brown stems. Seventy years later Fred couldn't quite recall precisely which variety stole the Temple Show. But steal the Show they did. The caladiums – *Fred's* caladiums as he now considered them – were awarded a Gold Medal. Suddenly all those hours he had spent with the crocks and the moss and the temperature soaring close to the enervating eighties seemed immensely purposeful hours. How wise he'd been to choose gardening as his life's work!

Fred would never admit to a downright love of London. He was far too much the countryman for that. But whenever our discussions turned to those proving days in the King's Road, there was a note of wistful affection in his voice as he remembered some of the missions that had been entrusted to him.

Ever since that memorable occasion of *The Seats of the*

Mighty, he had warmed to the excitement of a First Night in a London Theatre. So when flowers – magnificent flowers – were wanted to deck the foyer on another First Night, Fred became infected with that sense of occasion as he hailed a 'growler', bundled his assortment of roses and cyclamen and cinerarias aboard, and headed for the Strand or Drury Lane. One way and another, he was getting a taste for the theatre!

Society weddings and 'coming out' parties were another source of big business for Veitch's – and of work for Fred.

"Back in those days," he told me, "those folk in high society didn't half go the pace. No sooner was one party over than they were planning another big 'do'. Off I'd go with a couple of flower arrangers and sometimes we'd work right through the night just to make sure everything was bright and beautiful by the time the first guests arrived."

It was the rule rather than the exception for the flower arrangers to be battling hard against the clock, so intricate were the designs demanded but so brief the time allowed to complete them. The final touches would be added as the Head Butler hovered imperiously between hallway and banqueting room and the kitchen staff waited impatiently in the wings.

Fred and his hard pressed team would leave by one door while the guests arrived by another, and on nights like these Fred would have a fleeting glimpse of gracious living. Briefly, through an uncurtained window, he would see the laden table he had helped to decorate and watch the punch being served into crystal goblets that shimmered with a splendid opulence. But this was as close as he came to the London of leisure and luxury. His wages made no concessions to extravagant living and, after he had paid his weekly lodging bill, the change remaining was no burden to his pocket.

"Luckily," he reflected, "I was never a great eater. But I knew what I liked . . . and in those days I was extra keen on good old sausage and mash. Just as well too . . . because I

37

found one little shop near my lodgings where you could get a great big helping of sausage and mash for only twopence. So on a Saturday night I'd treat myself to that and go back to my lodgings well satisfied."

Among his room-mates Fred made few friends. It wasn't merely that he had little to say to them. He didn't much care for them either.

"Seems to me, looking back," he admitted, "that they all had some sort of failing Frank. They either snored . . . or they swore . . . or they even smelt a bit! And that didn't appeal to me at all."

Not knowing Fred in those days, it is difficult for me to diagnose the reasons for this lack of communication; unwholesome habits were probably only half the cause. My guess is that the basic shyness I often detected in Fred was with him in greater measure as a youngster; he never courted popularity in an overt way though he valued the many friendships he made.

By way of mental escape from the unlovely London lodging house, he would remind himself that the Surrey Hills and the Sussex Downs were only a few miles from Chelsea. They seemed so distant now. Yet he'd walked that road from London to Reigate in a single night. He could leap on a train and soon be back in Reigate or Pulborough if only he had the money for the fare; and if only he had the courage to admit that he was just a little home-sick.

As the London Spring gave way to Summer he would reflect on the changing seasons down in Sussex by the sea. The little festival of bluebells and primroses would be over now. Today the golden rock-roses and the wild columbine would be waiting in the wings ready for their moment of high-summer glory. But these thoughts were getting him nowhere.

He must stay in Chelsea and endure the failings of his room-mates until word came of a really worth-while position. After all, his foreman at Veitch's was willing now to give him a warm recommendation; his successes with the caladiums at the Temple Show were still fresh in his memory. And soon precisely the chance he'd longed for came his way – the chance to return to 'private practice' as some of the gardeners called it.

A post was on offer at Hedsor Park, the seat of Lord Boston near Cliveden in Buckinghamshire – and here he would be in charge of a conservatory and several greenhouses.

When Fred presented himself for his interview at Hedsor, he did detect a mild reluctance to show him precisely what might be in store for him, but he dismissed this as a natural reticence to whet his enthusiasm before he'd actually been accepted for the job.

In fact, although Fred accepted the appointment and delighted in the prospect of escape from those unending London pavements, a sense of foreboding seemed to grip him from his very first day at Hedsor.

Watering the parched conservatory early that first morning, he succeeded in swamping the breakfast-table in the nearby servants hall. That was just the beginning of his troubles. The same evening, when invited to play billiards in the servants' club room, his cue went straight through the baize to the dumbfounded disbelief of his fellow players. They said nothing, but their withering glances said all.

This was the last game of billiards Fred ever played – though he did admit that, years later, he made good use of a billiard cue to stake a particularly strong growing plant. In any event, Fred's errant billiard cue served also as his pointer back to London, though he never would tell me whether he left Hedsor at the Head Gardener's behest or whether he handed in his notice at the end of that first eventful month. However, he did agree that the way those gardens were run was as big a puzzle to him as the giant *Araucaria Imbricata* or monkey puzzle tree for which Hedsor Park was famous.

He admitted too that Hedsor had taught him the lesson that no gardener should accept a new post until he has seen at first hand the soil that will be his to work and the plants that will be his to cultivate; not to mention the company he will be expected to keep!

"It's like going to live with a family without any idea how you'll hit it off with them," Fred observed. "But I'll tell you this much. They'd been kind enough to keep my old job warm for me in Chelsea – and going back there was just like going back home. Those chaps in the King's Road gave me a lovely welcome and never asked what had gone wrong down at Hedsor Park. But the first opportunity I had for a quiet word with my boss I said to him 'Before I take another job, I think I'll ask your advice, Sir'. And he simply said 'Right Streeter. I know the sort of job you're looking for and I'll keep my eyes open for you.'"

Fred's foreman was as good as his word. He put him in charge of a new group of plants to widen his field of experience – the *crotons* of the *euphorbia* family and the *dracaena*. He would set aside time (always at a premium in a busy nursery) to discuss the finer points of plant-care with Fred and to answer his seemingly unending string of questions. He even helped him in the search for new lodgings, for Fred had settled once again in a house with a dungeon-like basement where meals were eaten in semi-darkness and where the air was never totally free from the scent of rancid fat.

"What a morning it was Frank when that foreman called me into his office and said he'd spotted just the sort of job to suit me."

First he told Fred of the star attractions of the job he had in mind. The Head Gardener was a splendid fellow – highly respected in the business, with years of experience to his credit, and a most pleasant man to have as a boss. As for the gardens themselves – these were among the finest of their particular region . . . the sort of gardens in which Fred could truly be proud to serve. But the foreman saved until last the two not-so-promising aspects of the job he had in mind:

"The wages will be fifteen shillings a week – a bit less than you're getting now. But don't let that worry you. The bothy and all your meals are thrown in!"

Fred swallowed hard, tried to muster a responsive smile, but before he could reply, his chief was speaking again.

"One other thing. It'll mean going across the water. Never mind Streeter. That will be grand experience for you. Take my tip. This is just the job for you."

Fred had asked for advice and now he must take it. If the path of progress lay overseas – then over the water he must go!

IV

"Flowers are just like human beings. They thrive on a little kindness. But treat them harshly and they'll soon start to wilt and fade."

This was one of Fred Streeter's firmly held beliefs – a belief that few of his listeners could bring themselves to challenge. But when he earnestly suggested that they should *talk* to their flowers as well, there were many who said he was endowing the plant world with altogether too much humanity. Before we knew it Fred would be insisting that everything was so lovely in the garden that there was no such thing as a weed!

This was perfectly true. Fred's definition of a weed was a herb that Providence had planted in the wrong place. Consult the dictionaries and you will find that they come up with much the same answer; their definition of a weed is: 'a wild herb springing where it is not wanted'.

"Take the old stinging nettle," Fred would say. "Alot of

folk think that its only job in life is to give them a jolly painful warning if they're trespassing in a farmer's field. But
have you ever tried eating it in a salad – good and early in
the year when it's nice and young? More tasty than lettuce
you know. And even when the leaves are fully grown you
can cook them just like spinach. Lots of people did that
during the War . . . and suddenly discovered what they'd
been missing all these years!"

Fred had plenty of time for the thistle too.

"Fancy calling that a *weed*," he would say with a hint of
despair. "Those people up in Scotland certainly knew what
they were doing when they chose the thistle as their em-
blem. If you don't believe me, take a really close look at the
very next thistle you see. Beautifully shaped leaves . . .
lovely red or purple flowers . . . and a delicate covering that
has such a wonderfully light and airy name. Thistledown!"

No doubt about it: inspired by a topic really close to his
heart, Fred could wax lyrical at times. And it was this same
romantic streak in his character which had responded on
that memorable morning at Veitch's of Chelsea when he
had learnt the news of a probable job 'across the water'.
Those very words had the heady tang of excitement. And
when the foreman had urged him to seize this new opportunity without delay, he had added – "We'll miss you here
Streeter. You've worked hard. You've got on well with the
other lads . . . but now it's time for you to get out into the
world a bit. And I'm sure you'll enjoy it over there in Ireland!"

Ireland ?

So . . . that job across the sea wasn't to take him to some
far-flung outpost of Empire as the foreman's words had
rather suggested. There were to be no glimpses of Oriental
Gardens for Fred, no journeys through olive groves, no in-
structional visits to tea plantations in distant Assam. Those
words 'across the sea' had promised such a wealth of excitement. But on second thoughts – even a trip to Ireland

43

seemed scarcely less exciting for a young man who had never before left England's shores. It was indeed a journey to Straffan House in County Kildare where not only was the Head Gardener held in high esteem but where the owner herself – the Honorable Mrs. Barton – was a gardener of talent and imagination.

At this moment I am consulting some notes Fred wrote for me in his own hand. He prepared them at the time I first suggested we should write a book together; and here he describes in his still firm hand his first glimpse of the splendid gardens of Straffan.

> "Oh what a garden, far greater and better than any I had ever seen – and this was my turning point. I had good Christian mates all keenly interested in their work – and here I was taught to raise my hat to ladies."

The plain truth was that Fred had precious little time to meet the ladies in those days. The mere size of his job was daunting. The gardens of Straffan seemed to stretch to the horizon and beyond. Huge walls divided the specialist sections of the gardens and, trained obediently across those walls, were some of the most impeccably tutored trees Fred had ever seen. Apricots . . . peaches . . . cherries. Nature certainly seemed to smile on Straffan. One specially favoured pear tree had over thirty different varieties grafted upon it.

If today we think of Fred Streeter as the last of a vanished race of gardeners, then the Head Gardener at Straffan was again in a class apart. His name was Fred Bedford and Fred Streeter once painted a colourful word picture of his first meeting with the man he came to admire and respect.

"First off he looked like a real toff to me Frank. Kid gloves, bowler hat – even spats I believe. Imagine him being

44

a gardener! You could never imagine that he'd ever dirtied his hands in his life . . . let alone done anything *really* mucky like lifting potatoes or putting soot on the celery. And he had a habit of dusting down his sleeve with his hand as though a speck of soil had fallen on to it. Yet he was a very clever man you know and a man you could take your troubles to."

Among the staff at Straffan House Fred Bedford was known as the Skipper; and he was in every way a gardener in the grand manner. Even the Skipper's more modest flower beds would be twenty feet deep, and some of his dividing walls were close on a quarter of a mile long. He liked space, he liked air – yes, even perhaps a hint of drama in his gardens. Surely it was here that his pupil Streeter developed the habit of giving plants plenty of space to breathe and plenty of territory in which to spread their roots.

Fred never approved of the thick sowing of seeds or the crowding of plants in too great a profusion. Only lawn seed and mustard and cress should be sown thickly, he said. He liked colourful variety it is true, but ordered variety in the Straffan tradition.

Yet as Fred was soon to discover, not everything was flourishing at Straffan. The old vinery he was set to clear and prune was in a desperately sorry state; and as he launched himself into the task, working meticulously along the line of houses, the Skipper was discreetly watching him day by day. Few words were exchanged but Fred was well aware that he was being assessed.

"*He* knew that *I* knew he was watching me," chuckled Fred. "But we never admitted it to each other. Still . . . when some lovely bunches of fruit eventually started to appear and that terrible old vinery began to look quite pretty again, he *did* say I'd done a nice job. My pruning had been good and firm. And I'd kept the crop down to a sensible level."

Mark you, Fred and the Skipper didn't always see eye to

eye. It was the Skipper's belief that one of the biggest mistakes in the gardening book was to feed developing strawberries with manure. It did nothing much to aid their growth and it gave a nasty, musty taste to the strawberries. At least, so *he* said!

Fred had been reared in a different school – and as the Straffan strawberries swelled and ripened, he slowly stepped up his secret doses of mild manure water. He knew full well that, as strawberries mature, they can almost be killed with kindness; he knew in particular that too much nitrogen can cause untold damage. But he also knew from first-hand experience that a modest dressing of manure can make a sizeable difference to the crop. And it was indeed a most handsome crop he presented at length to the well pleased Mr. Bedford.

"Lovely fruit," said Mr. Bedford, selecting himself a rich, ripe strawberry. Then popping it into his mouth he added – "Lovely flavour too. Just goes to show that there's no need at all for that wretched manure water some folk use."

Fred smiled to himself and kept his own counsel. "It simply taught me another lesson Frank," he said, "that even the best of gardeners don't always agree!"

Yet although he was first to admit that the traditional picture of a gardener as "a cussed old chap who won't listen to anyone else's opinions" is often close to the mark, he also maintained that gardening is one of those occupations in which you are the eternal apprentice. The days of learning are never over; and when Fred learned that the nearby Gardens of Trinity College, Dublin were a positive cornucopia of delights for the dedicated gardener, he decided they must surely have something to teach him. Not only were the glasshouses of Trinity held in high esteem – but they were also particularly proud of the *Gunnera chilensis* that flourished there. This plant – a native of Australasia – will cheerfully grow up to eight feet tall, with leaves of a six-foot span; and, on his first visit, as Fred stood in awe beside this giant from 'down under', he resolved to return to the Gardens again and again to explore their wonders in depth.

It was on one of these visits that he was introduced to Professor Burbidge, a much respected figure in the horticultural world. He warmed to Fred's quiet sincerity and sensed in this earnest young gardener with the unfamiliar Sussex accent a man who meant to get on in his chosen career. Together they would walk through the Gardens discussing some finer point of plant-care – a strangely assorted couple in one sense, yet very much at one in their love of plants.

The Professor was a regular house guest at Straffan and soon he was having a quiet word with Mrs. Barton – the Lady of the House – suggesting that Streeter had such a flair for the more exotic side of gardening that he might be just the man to put in charge of her Orchid House.

The promotion was made and a friendship developed from which, by his own admission, Fred Streeter learnt many things. In particuar he was taught the correct technique of potting orchids; and whenever he knew the Professor was due to visit Straffan, he would busy himself collecting the pots and the materials so that the job should progress with the quiet efficiency that Professor Burbidge applied to every task in greenhouse and garden.

He favoured large clay pots for the orchids; and he liked them half filled with sizeable crocks – insisting that both pots and crocks should be thoroughly sterilised before the delicate potting ritual got under way.

As for compost, the Professor prescribed a blend of osmunda fibre and sphagnum moss. These two ingredients had to be finely chopped and then thoroughly mixed together; and as Fred prepared this vital blend, the Professor would sniff the air appreciatively, rather in the manner of an hotelier approving the skills of his head chef.

Finally – like every true specialist in the rarified world of

47

orchids – the Professor stressed with an almost religious fervour that the placing and settling of the orchids into their new home were tasks for a firm yet supremely delicate hand.

The secret, of course, is to settle the anchor roots in the mixture without the slightest hint of damage – yet to make those roots so firm that if you lift a single leaf of the plant, you lift the pot as well. Finally, with the help of a small peg – in goes the remainder of the mixture so that it forms a snug cocoon around the whole plant. It may all sound tolerably simple but the expert will tell you that it *is* an art . . . and one which Professor Burbidge had mastered. Before long, his pupil Fred Streeter had mastered it too!

"Seems to me," said Fred, "that we chaps didn't grow up half as fast in those days as young fellows do now. Remember, I'd celebrated my twenty-first birthday when I was over there in Ireland . . . and of course that made me a man! But lots of the older men still called me 'boy' or 'lad' even though I was in charge of those orchid houses. So I thought to myself – the time has come to do something about this. It's time I really grew up."

'Doing something about it' could mean only one thing . . . to seek and find another job. It must be a job with an added measure of responsibility . . . and a job where no longer could that somehow derogatory tag of 'boy' be applied to him; and since Fred still held in warmest affection his home counties of Sussex and Surrey, the prospect of a foreman's job in neighbouring Hampshire was very attractive.

Fred penned his application for the post in his flowing copperplate hand, listing his now quite impressive range of experience and hinting with a becoming modesty that his training in many fields might fit him for the title of foreman.

"They'd told us at school," Fred remembered, "how to write off for jobs. Never to scratch out a word if you make a mistake – but to start the whole blinking thing over again. And never to sound too cocky! Say what you can do with honesty – then leave it at that."

Fred's honest letter produced the desired result, for soon he learnt the news that he was to exchange the tag of 'boy' for the title of foreman. It was goodbye to Ireland and back to the familiar South of England. And though he had many regrets at leaving Straffan, it was the challenge of his new appointment that was occupying his thoughts as he crossed the turbulent Irish Sea one night in March 1901 – destination Basing Park near Alton.

"I don't remember much about the journey down to London" Fred admitted. "I was so caught up with my own thoughts that I didn't have any time to admire the scenery. But I do remember I'd been promised that someone from the big house would be waiting for me at Alton Station; and sure enough there he was as I staggered off the platform with all my cases – a splendid looking chap with a great big top hat and the smartest horse and trap you ever saw!"

The coachman's first words of greeting brought only a gruff response from the new foreman gardener. Kindly enquiries about Fred's journey over from Ireland met with little more success. But the driver was no man to be easily defeated. He knew it would pay him well to strike up an early acquaintance with the taciturn character who sat beside him, since a bond of friendship with the foreman gardener was also a passport to a ready supply of garden produce. So now he turned to his favourite topic – women . . .

"The place we're passing now is a laundry," he said with an elegant wave of his whip. "Two nice young girls live there – all alone with mother! Should think that girls like that need a man's company – eh?"

There was an icy pause before Fred replied – "Girls? I'm not interested in *girls*. Gardening is my job!"

The remainder of the journey passed in silence. There

seemed nothing more to say; but on arrival at Basing Park the driver held a hasty conference with his cronies – warning them that the new foreman gardener didn't talk, didn't laugh – and worst of all had no time for women.

It was a damning trio of failings for any newcomer; and Fred's reputation as a woman hater gained in credence when, a few days later, plans were being laid for a staff dance. Politely but without enthusiasm Fred was invited to attend, but he had to admit that he didn't dance a single step.

"See what I mean?", said the now convinced coachman. "We've got a strange one here." And such conviction went into his words that it was soon agreed that Fred Streeter was one of those men who live for work and never allow a chink of warmth to show through their armour.

Yet if Fred was slow to make friends at Basing Park, he was quick to sense that there was a wealth of opportunity here. Not that the gardens were flourishing; quite the reverse. The soil had a sadly defeated look to it, and the men who now came under his charge moved about their tasks as though stricken with the palsy. The vineries were run down and unproductive; the borders were unimaginative and overgrown; and although (to Fred's delight) there was an orchid house here, the plants seemed just as dispirited as the men who tended them.

"Yet the fact remained," Fred insisted, "that there were all sorts of possibilities here – and that's what you want to look for whenever you move to a new garden. Never mind that things have been neglected. Never mind if you can't imagine how all the work is ever going to get done. You'll find the time all right, providing you can spot those possibilities!"

A new generation of flowering shrubs was urgently needed at Basing Park, so Fred detailed a group of men for trenching duty. New windbreaks were needed too, so Fred settled for *Rhododendron ponticum* as a quick and colourful means of lending a new element of shelter to the bleakness of the Park. And true to the Straffan tradition, he decided to plan his borders in the grand manner. Fully sixty feet those borders should be — and filled with an exciting company of syringas, magnolias, azaleas and philadelphus.

Meantime, in one of the Basing Park hothouses, Fred made a memorable discovery. They even grew *pineapples* here.

"Cooor," said Fred, "I wished my old friend the Professor could have been with me then. He liked anything that was just that little bit out of the ordinary. You see, I knew next to nothing about pineapples — and I'd have dearly loved his advice."

Mark you, no one could blame the new foreman gardener for admitting that he was ignorant of this particular fruit. There are close on a thousand different species and — as the learned books will tell you — the pineapple is both epiphytic and xerophytic.

Perhaps that leaves you just as baffled as I was the first time Fred broke the news to me. It simply means that the pineapple plants make their home on other vegetation without robbing their hosts of their goodness — and that they can cheerfully withstand long periods of drought, when they lapse into a semi-dormant state. Some plants in this family even form little cups with their leaves in order to provide themselves with their own means of taking a drink.

"Yes, they're fascinating things those pineapples," said Fred. "And when you're potting them out, be specially careful about the drainage. You want to use nice loose loam to grow them in and to crock them up with broken bricks and a few bits of charcoal. Over at Basing, once I'd potted them all up, I'd put them in a bed of sawdust because that laps up the moisture quick as a flash, just as soon as it has drained through the pots."

Fred welcomed work of this sort — work which gave him

51

ample scope to experiment with new methods and new materials; but he dared not devote too much time to the pineapple house and the orchid house and the other exotic elements in the garden when so much had yet to be accomplished outside.

He had arrived at Basing Park when the March winds were still insisting that this was winter-time in Hampshire. The Spring of 1901 gave way to a golden summer while Fred toiled on. And though, with the coming of Autumn, the fruit borders had been licked into shape, the flower borders had blossomed, and even an uneasy truce had been declared between the dandified driver and the taciturn foreman gardener — any thoughts of recreation seldom crossed Fred's mind.

"You've got to remember Frank," Fred would stress, "That those were days when you didn't only have to prove that you were man enough to get a really good job. You had to show that you were capable of holding it! This was the first time in my life I'd had a tidy number of men actually working for me; and I meant to set them an example by working almost every hour God sent."

Almost every hour . . . but not quite. Fred's Sunday morning visit to church was something he would never neglect, no matter how insistent the garden's needs might be; and on Saint Patrick's Day 1902, the church service over, he decided to take the luxury of a stroll in the country. The Polytechnic had schooled him well and his 'strolls' had the habit of developing into marathons.

When Fred first told me that *this* was the most momentous walk he ever took in his life, I was tempted to think this was perhaps a colourful turn of phrase without too much substance. But he soon convinced me.

"I suppose I'd gone about three or four miles Frank through some lovely country when I spotted a signpost saying that I was getting close to a litttle village called Froxfield. Then suddenly, when I was passing what seemed to be a smallish thatched farmhouse, I noticed at the gate an elderly lady and a girl, deep in conversation – like the ladies love to do! They didn't see me, but I saw them and I somehow guessed they might be mother and daughter."

Fred smiled at the thought and, refreshing his memory after a space of seventy years, he continued: "Now I'll always recall what the girl was wearing Frank. It was a white blouse, a black skirt – and the skirt was all covered in dog's hairs. Of course, the dog was there as well – it kept jumping up at her and barking. But although I was a shy sort of fellow in those days I raised my hat and said 'Good afternoon everybody' and then bent down and patted the dog – even though it was a blessed nuisance!"

An elderly gentleman (the owner of the house), joined the group at this stage; and while the newcomer engaged the other lady in discussion, Fred turned his attentions to the younger member of the party. Weren't the daffodils lovely, he remarked – and wasn't this a frisky little dog.

"Didn't seem to matter," Fred recalled, "That our conversation wasn't really getting us anywhere. It was pleasant enough to be in this girl's company. And I soon discovered that, just as I'd guessed, the lady with her *was* her mother, while it was the old chap who owned the cottage."

At this point the girl consulted her watch and decided it was time to be getting home for tea.

"Quick as a flash, I had another inspiration," said Fred.

"'Can I push your bike for you?' I asked – and away we went down the lane, leaving the other two still deep in conversation at the cottage gate."

During that brief stroll, Fred quietly took stock of the girl he described as 'the loveliest young lady I had ever seen'. She was tall. She was fair. And Fred was quick to notice that her eyes were what he called 'a tender blue'.

Her name was Hilda Burden. She was a teacher at the local school; and – still more significantly from Fred's point of view – she was the daughter of the Head Game Keeper at

Basing Park.

"He was a positive giant of a man," said Fred, addressing his words to Heaven. "Six feet four if he was an inch. I couldn't believe that this girl at my side was his daughter. But on that stroll back to her home I kept looking to see if she was wearing an engagement ring . . . and though I was pretty sure she wasn't, I thought I'd make doubly sure."

"Are you engaged?", Fred enquired as they arrived at her house.

"No – I'm not engaged," replied Hilda.

"Then may I see you again?" Fred asked with growing boldness.

Hilda smiled.

"Yes, I'd like that," she said. "I shall be going to church tonight. I'll look out for you there."

Perhaps for the first time in his career, Fred faced the problem of divided loyalties. Looking at life through the eyes of his employer, who had entrusted so many men to his care, there could be no doubt that the first duty lay with the gardens of Basing Park. He had worked diligently for just such a job as this. Now he must prove his worth. Yet the moment his thoughts turned to Hilda, his resolve to spend every waking hour in the garden was carried away like dandelion seed on a high summer breeze.

The change in Fred was especially noticeable as each working day drew to a close. Here was no silent foreman plodding into the bothy, bluntly enquiring whether the mowing machines had been properly oiled and the greenhouse temperatures faithfully logged – then going his own unsmiling way without another word. Now he would come whistling into the bothy, change with unaccustomed speed into his best suit (which was also his only suit); pull on his brown boots, polished to the shine of a new season's chestnut; and away he would go down the drive with the rhapsodic prospect of an evening in the company of the fair-haired, blue-eyed Hilda.

"Coor, isn't love wonderful," said Fred to me once with his usual directness. "I knew right off that there'd never be another girl in my life. Priceless she was Frank. Though talking of prices, did I ever tell you of the time I went shopping in Portsmouth to buy her a Christmas present?"

Fred had decided that Hilda would look her best with a splendid fur about her neck and a muff to match. So in he went to one of Portsmouth's largest stores, and when the assistant asked him how much he wished to spend on the purchase he replied reassuringly – "Now don't you worry about the price miss . . . I simply want the very best you have."

Brave words. But, as Fred admitted, he was in for a surprise when the assistant returned a minute or two later with a fur of splendid sheen across one arm and a deeply luxuriant muff clasped in her hand.

"I think you'll find these just the thing sir," she said. "Fifty guineas the two."

"Talk about wanting to drop!" said Fred. "I wished the ground would gobble me up – because I'd only got five pounds to my name. So I told the assistant how I was placed . . . and away she went again. But what a sigh of relief I breathed when back she came with a really lovely fur and muff for just five pounds!"

The crisis safely over, Fred carefully counted out the notes. The meagre handful of coins still remaining in his pocket was just enough for a cup of tea and a bun at the stall outside the station before he returned triumphantly to Basing Park.

Triumph it was – for Hilda delighted in that Christmas gift, just as certainly as her mother was beginning to delight in Fred. She liked the serious approach to life of this earnest young man. She liked his politeness. She liked the soberness of his dress. In fact, there was only one thing that did not win her unstinting praise. It was Fred Streeter's beard.

55

With the way that mothers have, Mrs. Burden communicated her feelings to Hilda. In turn, Hilda communicated them to Fred.

That night, back in the bothy, Fred stropped his cutthroat razor to the keenest edge it had ever known, whipped up a mountainous cream of lather in his shaving mug and with sure, firm strokes removed his beard.

On Christmas morning Hilda Burden attended church. She was wearing, a shade self-consciously, a very new muff. On one side of her stood her mother; on the other, ram-rod straight, stood a clean-shaven Fred Streeter.

"Mark you," said Fred recalling that memorable Christmas Day, "I was never one to rush things. You've probably noticed that! And although we wanted to get married right away, we talked things over for hours on end and decided that I had to be earning quite a bit more before I could take on all the responsibilities of a married man. So when I heard that a Member of Parliament was looking out for a new chap by way of a managing foreman – I decided that *he* might be the chap for me. Only I'd reckoned without that perishing hailstorm!"

"Hailstorm?" I enquired. "How did a *hailstorm* come into all this?"

The answer was simple enough. Fred's new appointment was to take him to Barham Court near Maidstone where Sir Charles Warde (a man of razor-sharp wit and equally cutting tongue) had his home. Sir Charles was Member of Parliament for the Medway Division of Kent and took particular pride in the range and quality of fruit that was grown at Barham Court. Unhappily the gardens had recently been ravaged by quite the fiercest hailstorm in living memory.

Glass had been smashed in an orgy of destruction from the skies. Torrents of water had sent tons of topsoil swirling away from the gardens. Local people had cowered in their houses, convinced that those mammoth hailstones must

56

surely pierce the very tiles on the roof – while the one or two brave spirits who ventured out that terrible night had come back with chilling stories of hailstones as large as cricket balls and eerie lights in the sky that breathed impending doom.

All this happened some time before Fred arrived at Barham Court, but to him fell the task of repairing the ravages.

"Seems to me," said Fred, "That we put in acres of new glass there and slapped on hundreds of gallons of paint to get the houses back into shape again. But old Sir Charles wasn't half as worried about his greenhouses as he was about his blessed strawberries. And do you know Frank, that very same year we grew a couple of thousand strawberry plants in six-inch pots. What a sight they were. Good enough for the Lord Mayor of London."

In fact the man who had just completed his term as Lord Mayor – Sir Marcus Samuel – paid a visit to Barham Court to see Fred's strawberries. And he was not all that amused at what he saw, for there existed between Sir Charles and Sir Marcus a supposedly friendly (yet often fierce) rivalry as to who could produce the better fruit. Sir Marcus was a lavish spender on his garden and – in view of the hailstorm – had written off the competition from Barham Court as no longer a threat to his supremacy. Fred Streeter's arrival changed all that. His Royal Sovereigns were magnificent – too magnificent for Sir Marcus's taste. He summoned his own Head Gardener and uttered the harshest words a Head Gardener is likely to hear.

"They've got a new managing foreman over at Barham Court," he announced. "Name of Fred Streeter."

"Never heard of him Sir," replied the gardener bluntly.

"Well you've heard of him now," said the tight-lipped Sir Marcus. "And from all accounts he could teach you a

57

lesson or two."

A day or two later, that ill-used Head Gardener was despatched to Barham Court; and though his mission was never defined in as many words, its purpose was plain enough. To learn from Fred Streeter the finer points of strawberry culture.

For Fred it was more of a triumphal procession than a simple tour of the glasshouses. Yet his days in the service of Sir Charles (though crowned with successes at many a show), did not bring him the opportunities he was really seeking. He wanted a larger territory for his domain. He wanted a boss who would listen more sympathetically to his recommendations. He wanted, most of all, that magical title of Head Gardener – with all the rewards and responsibilities it entailed. Which is why sad news from across the Irish Sea proved, in a sense, good news for Fred Streeter.

The news was from Straffan House, saying that Mrs. Barton's husband had only a few weeks to live and that, with his death, she could no longer maintain the huge estate in Co. Kildare. She would be moving to Birtley House at Bramley in Surrey. Could she look to Fred Streeter as her new Head Gardener? Word had somehow reached Ireland that Fred had marriage in mind. If this were so, would he be interested in the cottage that would be on offer to the new Head Gardener?

"Of course, I was upset to hear the news of my old boss," said Fred. "I'd had some happy times at Straffan and I didn't like the thought of sadness over there. But I've got to admit Frank that this was just the opportunity I'd been waiting for. A better paid job . . . and a place where Hilda and I could set up home."

On January 10th 1906 Hilda and Fred were married at Privett Church near Alton. Hilda's father had promised the villagers a pint of beer all round on the day of his daughter's wedding – and he was as good as his word. But for Hilda and Fred there was to be no honeymoon; he was back at work the very next day.

"Do you know Frank," he admitted, "we never did have a honeymoon. But then, who needs a honeymoon when you've picked the right job – *and* the right young lady?"

V

"Oh those blessed blackbirds. I've got no time for them Frank. They'll ruin your lettuces . . . they'll pinch your peas. And as soon as your cauliflower starts making its curd, they'll be after that too!"

Fred Streeter had few enemies. I suppose they could be numbered on the fingers of one hand. Blackbirds . . . slugs . . . wireworm . . . greenfly. And of course the detested blackfly.

Just as he prescribed the simple expedient of sprinkling dry, powdered soil over the blackfly, so he would have an earthy way of dealing with most of the other uninvited guests in the garden. His formula for trapping slugs, for instance, was to place half a scooped-out orange or grapefruit face downwards in their likely path, and then to await results.

"They'll climb inside all right," explained Fred, "But they haven't got the sense to climb out again. And when

60

you go down the garden next morning, I'll bet you won't half be surprised when you lift up those grapefruit peels and see how many you've caught!"

For earwigs Fred had an equally down-to-earth answer; either an inverted jar perched on top of a short bamboo cane; or, more intriguingly, a half-open matchbox stuffed with dry grass and cunningly lodged in the foliage of the affected plants. Here again, although you would expect the visitors to go into reverse and clamber out again, somehow their minds don't work that way.

"But don't forget," Fred would remind his listeners, "one of the best weapons for fighting those blessed pests is the good old hoe. Take leatherjackets for instance. If you've got a really bad attack of leatherjackets then you'll probably have to fork one of those proprietary powders into the soil to get rid of them. But haven't you noticed that you usually find leatherjackets where the ground's been neglected for ages? Soon as you start working it again and hoeing it regularly you let lots of lovely air into the soil and that's just what the old leatherjacket can't stand. He's off to pester someone else's garden!"

When Fred and Hilda set up home at Bramley in the early days of 1906 and work in the Birtley House Gardens really got into its stride, Fred found himself facing another pest which threatened death and destruction to the cinerarias he was planning to show in London. The enemy was leaf miner – the larvae of moths or weevils which feed on leaf tissues and go tunnelling greedily into the plant. Hence that name 'miner'.

Fred studied the problem in depth. He had already won an enviable reputation for cinerarias and had no intention that his good name should be sullied by a mean little predator which chose to settle on his prized plants. He knew of course that small scale attacks can be contained by picking off the damaged leaves and burning them; he also knew that the larvae can be crushed in their mines by a well-

61

applied thumb and forefinger. But he worked on the basis that prevention was better than cure, and since many of the plants were still in the process of establishing their roots, he fed them daily with mild liquid manure so that (just like a well nourished human) they would be better equipped to ward off infection.

"My plan worked pretty well as a matter of fact," said Fred with his accustomed modesty. "I'll never forget it! The afternoon before the Show was to open at the Horticultural Hall in Westminster, up we went in a van with three dozen plants . . . all looking lovely and all without a trace of those blessed pests. Course you can bet there was pretty fierce competition. But do you know, those cinerarias won me my very first medal from the R.H.S. And that was the first of quite a few!"

Those days spent briefly at Birtley House brought Fred many moments of triumph, reinforcing his belief that there is just as much excitement to be gained from gardening as from any other pursuit you care to name. The athlete in his dream-moments pictures himself on the prizewinner's rostrum. The author in his reveries sees his work in the bestsellers' roll of fame. The gardener, solitary in the greenhouse, can already hear the murmur of approbation as the judges gather admiringly around his exhibits.

Fred relished the excitement of the big Show. He revelled in the judges' confirmation that all those hours of patient, lonely labour had produced the finest plants in their class. Yet he was realist enough to acknowledge that most of life's triumphs have a counterbalancing moment of tragedy waiting in the wings, ready to make some untimely entrance.

The sadness came as Fred was drawing up his most ambitious plans for the Birtley House Gardens. His father, shortly past his fiftieth birthday, was suddenly taken ill with appendicitis. If those had been the days of antibiotics, the illness would probably have been little more than an unpleasant but short-lived incident. Instead, despite an emergency operation at Redhill Cottage Hospital, Fred's father died from pentonitis before the family could grasp the seriousness of his condition.

"I always felt a bit guilty about my father's death," Fred told me once. "I'd been so busy with my own life that I'd scarcely had time to set foot back home; and on my way back to Bramley from the funeral I began to think of all the things I might have done for him while he was still alive."

As it happened, Fred Streeter was to have little time to ponder his own and very personal bereavement. A few weeks later his employer at Birtley House – Mrs. Barton – confessed that she was suffering from a haunting depression that she could not escape. She set about the task of putting her affairs in order and very soon she took to her bed and died.

"Strange you know," said Fred, "The day I'd arrived at Bramley everything looked so bright and sunny. This was the very job I wanted . . . with a dear old lady to work for. But now everything looked black. She was dead – and so was my Dad. Still I couldn't help remembering what my mother had told me when I'd first left home. She'd tucked a Bible in my trunk – and on the flyleaf she had written 'Fear God, honour the King, and do unto others as you would that they do unto you'. And underneath she had added – 'You follow this my boy and you won't go far wrong'. She told me too that, no matter how bad things seem, we've still got a lot to thank God for. He produces everything, even the air we breathe . . . and if he stopped that we'd be done for, wouldn't we?"

Helped by this very practical side to his philosophy, Fred told himself that, with Mrs. Barton's death, a grey and melancholy chapter in his life had finally closed. With life's ineffable balance of light and shade, the next chapter must surely be brighter.

He must find a new garden with fresh challenges to offer;

and for some reason he could never even explain to himself, he felt a yearning to return to work in Ireland. Those had been good days with 'The Skipper' and the occasional visits to the gardens of Trinity College. But no suitable job presented itself across the water and, with a certain reluctance, he and Hilda moved instead to Liphook in Hampshire.

Here he was to be employed by Mrs. Barton's younger son, Harry Scott Barton, who had recently moved into Hewshott House. This was familiar territory, not many miles from the spot where eight years earlier Fred had first met the girl with the bicycle and had admired that host of daffodils!

"Mark you," Fred insisted, "I was to be Head Gardener once again. There was no going back now. But cooor . . . what a difference there was between this garden and the one I'd just left at Birtley. Over there, everything had been spick and span; scarcely a stone out of place. But this new garden was in a proper state – inside and out. And as a matter of fact Frank, the painters who were doing up our cottage there were pretty nearly the death of me."

The Streeters had settled into their new home while the painters were still at work; and not many weeks had passed at Hewshott before Fred was suffering from what he always described as a near-fatal attack of 'painter's colic'. Today, no doubt, the doctors would have a very different diagnosis for the complaint. It was almost certainly a deep seated virus infection to which the paint was merely an aggravating factor. In any event there was a spell during that first long winter at Liphook when the doctors came near to despairing of Fred's life, and throughout those unhappy days Hilda Streeter kept an almost constant vigil at her husband's bedside.

"I'd always been a great one for keeping fit and active you know," Fred remembered. "And this business of being flat on my back in bed didn't come at all easily to me. But I'll tell you one thing. It's at times like that you *really* know who your loved ones are . . . and, believe me, no one could have cared more lovingly for me than Hilda."

Harry Scott Barton was a man with a practical turn of mind and he soon realized that, even allowing for a reasonably swift and complete recovery, it would be many months before his Head Gardener would be back on full duties once again; so a temporary Head Gardener was appointed in his place while Fred (now convalescing), looked unhappily from his window as Spring gave way to Summer and all manner of tasks in the garden remained untouched.

"What a day it was," said Fred, "when at last I was able to get my gardening boots on again. Ask any *real* gardener and he'll tell you it's proper torture to be laid up when the garden's crying out for your attention. The weeds grow faster when you can't get at them and there's that much to do when you start again that it's difficult to know where to begin!"

But Fred knew precisely where to begin on his Hewshott House plans – and in the early days of a gentle Autumn his dreams of the rose gardens and the rockeries began at last to become a reality.

There were several other projects in the air. The creation of a new orchard in a stretch of parkland – and the making of a huge herbaceous border in which the massed ranks of plants were to produce such a spectacular variety of colours that even Fred admitted that this was one of the finest borders of its kind he had ever seen.

Yet still he had the gnawing doubt that the gardens of Hewshott lacked some vital ingredient to give them the hallmark of true originality. Then he hit on the answer. He would create here his first full-scale water garden!

The sound of water tumbling over stones has a musical magic all its own – a magic that need not even be denied to the owner of the relatively small garden. At Hewshott, Nature herself had provided the basic element – water – in great abundance; for there was a largish lake in the gardens and a river running close by. But even the far humbler garden usually has space for a modest pond; and there, of course, that aquatic extrovert, the water lily, will flourish.

Fred used the well known method of establishing his water lilies in open wicker baskets, but that was just the beginning of this particular success story. He had a host of other aquatics up his sleeve for his water garden and a special love of *Pontederia Cordata* with its long, bright green leaves and its spikey blue or white flowers.

When building that water garden at Hewshott, Fred remembered the lessons of Straffan and carefully avoided any hint of overcrowding.

"I'd already seen in other gardens Frank what can happen when you get too keen on the dear old water garden. You cram in an extra water lily here and another Bog Bean there. Then someone (likely the boss or the wife) says 'Can't we have some lovely sagittarias as well?' Before you know it your pond looks like Piccadilly Circus at the rush hour. So . . . you take my tip Frank. Don't crowd your pond with plants first off. Let Nature fill it up for you. Those water plants will grow like billyho in a year or two!"

A year or two was just about the time Fred stayed at Hewshott House. The date was 1911. Fred was nearly thirty-four years old; and while many people in the world of horticulture knew his name, he secretly felt that his talents should now be firmly linked with one of the finest gardens in the land. So when he heard that stately Lavington Park in Sussex was seeking a new Head Gardener it seemed possible that he was at last within reach of the post that would finally establish his reputation.

"It's always been my belief," Fred told me, "that first impressions are jolly important. And I'll never forget my first impression of the little fellow who was the Agent at Lavington Park. First off he said to me – 'Suppose I give you this job, I want to make it quite clear that you must never buy anything – not even a packet of seed or a penn'orth of string without getting my signature'."

"Coor I thought. That's taking things a bit far. So I said – 'Well I never buy string in penn'orths anyhow. I buy a dozen balls or so at a time, to be sure I never run out. But providing you'll buy the string for me, that'll save me a job and give me more time in the garden.' I could see his mind working Frank. He didn't know what to make of me, no more than I knew what to make of him. But at last he looked at me over his spectacles – *pince nez* I think you call them – and said 'You'll do Streeter. I'll see you have an interview with the master!'"

Those were still the days of the Master-Servant relationship; but Fred lost no time explaining to his master that the gardens here, though they had been well planned and skilfully handled, were still in need of special care. The soil was chalky; more loam was required to improve it. Shaded by the South Downs, this was a cold and windy spot throughout the winter months and therefore special skill was needed in drawing up a planting programme. On the credit side, the hot-houses of Lavington were prospering and as he saw their fine profusion of peaches and nectarines, of grapes and apricots, Fred's mind went back to Ireland and to those days of hot-house discussions with the Professor. With this new world of opportunity before him, how strange that his thoughts should still turn so often to Ireland! 'Forget it,' he told himself; 'there's no future for you there.' Yet somehow it wasn't as simple as that. The memories kept returning as he applied himself to the task of transforming Lavington Park into a still more memorable garden. Privately, he also set himself the task of winning a major award at the Chelsea Show.

"I decided that I'd specialise in showing Calceolarias Frank and I bought a packet of seeds to sow good and early in July. Now here's a trick that lots of folk don't know. When they start to germinate and you select the seedlings that you'll grow on, *don't* go for the strongest ones. That's all wrong. I know it sounds Irish but you want to select the weakest ones Frank. Give them a little encouragement and they'll come on all right, and they'll have far brighter colours than those great big sturdy fellows!"

And so it proved to be. Fred's calceolarias prospered. They were potted out, sprayed several times a day with soft water, and their numbers were finally reduced to a mere couple of hundred from which the show specimens would be selected. Then Fred adopted his much favoured technique of leaf feeding.

"Those calceolarias were so big and beautiful Frank," Fred recalled, "That the firm I'd bought the seed from came down to photograph them. They wanted to use the pictures in their catalogue. But then, just before the Show was due to open, I got a bit of a shock. The boss came round to see how they were getting on and he was so impressed with what he saw that he said to me – 'Forget about entering them in the Show Streeter. They're not going to London. I'm having them for myself.' Cooor Frank I could hardly believe my ears."

"Of course, Head Gardeners didn't have all that much authority in those days – and whatever the boss said was law. Never mind . . . I'd learned quite a lot about calceolarias as a result of all this. For instance, I'd been feeding those plants with regular doses of soot water and it taught me what a wonderful thing soot can be for the gardener. It doesn't only help to keep the slugs at bay – and of course the calceolaria is a real delicacy for those blessed slugs; but soot is also a marvellous fertiliser too. It acts just like a tonic to many plants – not only the flowering varieties like calceolarias but for many things in the vegetable garden as well, especially the good old onions!"

"Anyhow . . . my wonderful display of calceolarias never did get to Chelsea. But the owner certainly showed them off to all his friends – almost as if he'd grown them himself."

So Fred was denied what might have been one of his

greatest triumphs of all; but he hid his feelings. Men of the soil, he believed, had to learn to mask their emotions, yet secretly he began to question whether he was being adequately rewarded for all his efforts here at Lavington.

"I'd made some pretty big changes in the gardens there. And in spite of the business of the calceolarias, I'd managed to win quite a few medals for my boss. So since I was only getting twenty-five bob a week, and me a married man, I reckoned it was time to ask for a rise."

As protocol demanded, Fred made his application through the agent; and one can imagine how that gentleman's *pince-nez* must have misted over at the mere suggestion of a relatively new employee having the temerity to ask for a rise. But the message registered and at length Fred was summoned to a meeting with his employer where he was told that the request had been carefully considered and was indeed to be granted. His wages were to be increased by half-a-crown weekly! But when Fred insisted that this was not quite the rise he had in mind, there was a brief but crisp verbal exchange.

"Streeter," said the employer with weight, "no gardener is worth more than twenty-seven and six a week to me." And back he sat in his chair to let the force of his words sink in. There was a heavy pause before Fred replied with singular aptness – "And no employer who says that to me, Sir, is worth it either."

It would be easy, of course, to read a little too much into this story. To many of Fred's contemporaries, twenty-seven and six a week would have seemed a handsome wage. Even in the supposedly affluent South, nurserymen were still paying their trainee gardeners only five shillings a week – demanding that they worked a full twelve hour day right through the winter, and from six a.m. to eight p.m. during the summer months. Many of them had to send 'a little something' home each week, so if they were left with half-a-crown spending money, Fortune was treating them well. A

69

typical Head Gardener's wage would start around one pound weekly – and there are cases on record where this wage could be drastically reduced if the Gardener or one of his men was guilty of 'loss or damage' to tools or equipment . . .

There was also a heavy load of responsibility on the Head Gardener's shoulders. He was expected to keep a watchful, almost fatherly eye upon the welfare of his men; and no matter how favourable – or disastrous – the growing season might be, he was expected to present his employer with an unfailing succession of flowers and fruit and vegetables.

"It was no use," said Fred, "to explain to your boss that a particular crop had failed because the weather had been dead against you right from the start. He'd reply – 'I employ *you* to do the growing for me . . . so don't start giving me weak excuses about the weather."

In any event, Fred's days at Lavington were nearly over. He had never intended to settle there permanently, but for the first and only time in his career the mere matter of money had shaped a decision for him. He could no longer work for a man who placed such a modest price on his worth. Nor, when other men in the higher flights of gardening were earning much more, did he see why Hilda should have to work miracles each week to make her housekeeping money go round.

It was now 1913 and, although neither Fred nor Hilda shed a single tear at their departure from Lavington, they could not know that some of the blackest years of their lives were close at hand.

Briefly Fred worked as Head Gardener at a girls' boarding school near Watford; but his wistful thoughts of a return to Ireland still persisted, and when word arrived that the new owner of Straffan would like to have him in charge of the gardens, there were no doubts in Fred's mind about his decision.

He could scarcely wait to break the news to Hilda and she in turn grew more and more excited at the prospect of her first journey across the sea. Never mind that War had now been declared and, with Belgium already invaded, Britain was committed to the Allied cause. Never mind that some of the gloomy pundits were already saying that this was to be the bitterest and bloodiest war in the world's history. And never mind that even as they crossed the Irish Sea by the Night Mail there were rumours that a U-Boat was lurking ominously in their wake. Fred and Hilda were unashamedly happy, for new adventures and new opportunities lay ahead.

Yet this was to be a very different Straffan from the one Fred recalled with such affection. A casualty station had now been opened here. A unit of the Middlesex Regiment was entrenched in the Park; and soon, when the battle casualties began to flow in from France, it was Hilda Streeter rather than Fred who found that there were simply not enough hours in the day.

Even before leaving England she had been taking First Aid lessons. Now, as a member of the V.A.D., her skills were being called upon. Meanwhile Fred knew that his summons to the Army could not be long delayed so he set about training an older gardener to maintain some semblance of order in these once lovely gardens while he himself was away at the War.

"Of course Frank," Fred said, "Hilda and I both realised that I'd soon be on my way to France . . . and we did our best to prepare ourselves for the moment of parting. But somehow all the preparations in the world didn't make it any easier when the time arrived."

Army life did not come easily to Fred. Just as surely as he was a born gardener, he was not a born soldier. One July morning in 1915, on his first day in barracks at Bedford, he wrestled long and hard with cold water and a miserably blunt razor, trying to produce a shave that would satisfy

71

the granite-faced Orderly Sergeant. He did not succeed. Looking disbelievingly at poor Fred's stubbly chin he thrust his face close to Fred's and breathed with menace – "I can see we're going to have trouble with you old 'un!" And trouble wasn't far away.

Physically speaking, Fred was in splendid shape. Although his walking days with the Harriers were long since past, he could probably have marched that unlovable sergeant off his feet. It was simply that – right from the start – he could find no kinship with the Army's way of doing things; and his first glimpse of the Orderly Room at Bedford was a scene of such disorder that it lodged forever in his memory.

Even sixty years later that term 'Orderly Room' still conjured up a picture of a wretched bespectacled clerk poring over tea-stained papers and asking him improbable, impertinent questions about his life – questions that could have no relevance to the Hell on Earth that was waiting for him over the Channel. Fred could even recall the moist and yellowing cigarette that drooped from the fellow's lips, to be hastily removed and concealed at the approach of the Orderly Sergeant's clattering boots.

But like it or not, Fred Streeter was now in the Royal Fusiliers; and though, in years gone by, the mention of France had brought to mind evocative pictures of brightly-lit boulevards and girls of infectious gaiety, the France Fred saw in those early months of 1916 was the saddest, most sombre place he had ever looked upon. "Imagine it Frank," he said on one of those rare occasions when he would talk at any length about the First World War, "like any gardener worth his salt, I'd been brought up to think of the soil as something valuable . . . something to be treated like a friend. But in France the ground was all churned up – black and horrible; and here and there we'd stumble over the stump of an old tree sticking out of the ground. And everywhere of course there was that terrible smell of death."

It was during this particular conversation that I noticed for the first time a long white scar, standing out in strange relief on his cheek. Normally it was scarcely visible; but something – perhaps the memories evoked by our discussion that day – had made him touch it gingerly. I mentioned it to him; then quietly he told me the story of how, nearly sixty years earlier, he had come within an inch of death.

"That evening," he said, "we'd moved off from our base at Etaples and all through the night we'd marched closer and closer towards that terrible gunfire. Sometimes great flashes would light up the sky. Sometimes there'd be such a roar of gunfire that you were sure this was the end of everything. But it wasn't. We just marched on and on, with the rain getting heavier and heavier and our officer telling us to tie bits of old sacking over the mouths of our rifles to keep the barrels dry."

Though he told me this story sitting comfortably before the log fire in his home at Petworth, Fred's description was so realistic that I began to find myself trudging with him through that fearful night which was to have such a bloody ending.

"At last we came to a great long trench, Frank. We could just make it out in the light of those gun-flashes; and there we had our first bit of tragedy. One of my pals was climbing down into the trench when he missed his footing and went straight into a shell-hole. Now I was just behind him so I held out the butt end of my rifle to help him pull himself out. But no sooner had I done this than our officer gave me such a kick in the back that I nearly went sprawling. 'Don't you ever do anything like that again,' he warned me. 'The suction from that mud would have pulled both of you down.'"

That was the last glimpse Fred had of his comrade. Yet no sooner had he and the rest of his colleagues clambered safely down into the trench with the hope of snatching an hour's sleep, than the order came to attack. "This was a bayonet attack — a horrible thing. Of course this was my first taste of hand-to-hand fighting ... the first time I'd seen what war was really all about. And I'll tell you this Frank. I didn't like what I saw. It was just as though we'd stepped into Hell. They were all around us, shouting ... roaring... swearing. And it was every man for himself!"

Touching his cheek lightly as though the wound were still fresh Fred added — "Well that's where he got me Frank. Another inch higher and that would have been the end of me." Then he paused, giving me time to ask the inevitable question.

"Well, he wounded you Fred; but what happened to him?"

Fred smiled as he replied — "Don't worry Frank. I got him!"

This was the one occasion (almost certainly the only occasion) when I detected a revengeful note in Fred's voice; a sad illustration of what War can do to a man whose idea of Heaven is the soft tranquillity of a country garden.

There was little Fred could tell me about his journey back home from Flanders. Fever and delirium had given those particular memories a nightmare quality. But he did recall that, shortly before the bayonet attack, his thirst (heightened no doubt by trench fever) had been so intense that he had drunk water from a shell-hole full of dead soldiers. This had added a new element of infection to the fever which reached its height on the fearful, jolting train journey back to Base Hospital. Where and when he embarked for England he could not recall.

"I really only came to, Frank, when our hospital ship tied up at Southampton. We were given a lovely greeting there, then away we went on another train, bound for London. Now I remember during that train journey asking the M.O. in charge of us where we were going and he replied – 'It's the Middlesex Hospital for you my lad. They'll take good care of you there.'"

"Well going through London, Frank, I suppose I was still a bit delirious. But just for one moment I really thought I was in Heaven. One of those lovely little London flower girls came up to me and put a bunch of chrysanths on the stretcher. Then she bent down and kissed me and said 'You're all right now. You're back in England'. Well I thought she was an angel . . . I didn't think I was on this earth at all."

Fred's battles in Flanders may have been over. But his fight for life was beginning. For weeks in the Middlesex Hospital, where war casualties crowded every ward and the nurses were waging their own battles against sheer exhaustion, Fred slowly won his war against wounds and fever. Twelve months later he faced an examining doctor whose mission was to see whether this limping figure in hospital blue could be passed fit again for active service.

The verdict had a cold finality to it; Fred's papers were marked 'one hundred per cent disabled'. So clinically explicit were these words that for a moment Fred found himself wondering whether his only hope now was for a wheelchair existence and for the cloistered life of an invalid. But Fred Streeter still had nearly sixty years to live; and these were not to be the quiet potterings of a poor, disabled ex-serviceman but the colourful, kaleidoscopic life of a man who was to become Britain's most respected gardener – and one of our best loved broadcasters.

VI

"The soil is a wonderful thing Frank. Treat it like a good old friend . . . give it the sort of nourishment it really appreciates . . . keep it in good heart — and it will reward you by growing almost anything your heart desires!"

The soil of the Flanders fields had come near to breaking Fred's heart. It wore the same defeated look as the straggling columns of grey faced German soldiers who were soon to be making their way Eastwards . . . back to their unwelcoming homeland. Yet despite the bitter memories (and despite the doctor's gloomy predictions), Fred found plenty to be thankful for as the War came to an end. True the world was weeping and mourning its millions of sons; but this son of a Sussex shepherd was now launched upon a new battle, with the resourceful Hilda Streeter stoically at his side.

Hilda had spent many wartime months as a hospital nurse, returning later to Basing Park to care for her ailing father. She had a calm and a capable way with the sick and her skills were turned to good purpose when Fred at last was able to discard his hospital blue and enjoy the comforts of convalescence in a Hampshire country garden.

Some nights his sleep was tortured by dreams of dreadful realism that took him back to the blood-drenched battle-grounds. Some days he could scarcely walk a step without painful reminders that his wounds were far from healed. But in those closing months of 1918 – though Europe was gripped by a sense of apprehension at what the future might hold, Fred gained each day in confidence, telling himself with a quiet conviction that the invalid's chair was no place for a gardener. His place was with the plants and flowers . . . and soon Fred and Hilda were crossing the Irish Sea once again. The Head Gardener was returning to Straffan.

That title 'Head Gardener' sounds exalted. The pay that went with it was quite the reverse. It was thirty shillings a week; but if money was uncomfortably short, the tempers of many of the Irish folk were shorter still. They remembered too well the Easter Rebellion of 1916 with its shoot-ings and imprisonment of prominent members of Sinn Fein. They remembered the shelling of Dublin. And they remembered with an unforgiving bitterness that Fred Streeter had served in the English Army while his wife had helped with dedication to nurse the Army's wounded. Such a couple as this surely had no place in Ireland.

No longer at Straffan was there that easy relationship with other members of the staff which was still fresh in Fred's memory from pre-war days and which had prompted him to write – "I had good Christian mates, all keenly in-terested in their work."

These same men, now in the grip of nationalism, had enrolled in the service of Sinn Fein. And although there was an endless catalogue of jobs to be done in the gardens and greenhouses of Straffan if the neglect of the war years was to be repaired, Fred was beset with the problem of workers who had no heart for co-operating with an English Head Gardener and who arrived for their duties each morning exhausted and irritable. No wonder! They had spent half the night weapon training in one of the clandestine drill halls that were springing up everywhere; the other half had been devoted to sessions of indoctrination, about which the men maintained a tight-lipped silence.

Fred knew little – and cared less – about the political overtones of all this; he merely recognised that his position as the English Head Gardener of an important Irish estate was growing daily more unhealthy. He therefore determined to show his Irish colleagues that he wasn't just a good gardener – but a brilliant one! If they didn't care to co-operate with him, that was their bad luck. He would beat them at their own game.

"There was an old patch of ground at Straffan that the men said was good for nothing," Fred recalled. "So I told them there was no such thing as useless ground and for the next five years I'd grow potatoes there. You should have seen their faces. Telling an Irishman how to grow praties is like telling a man of Kent how to grow hops. They were pretty well certain I'd bitten off more than I could chew."

Fred gave that plot of ground the full Streeter treatment. He trenched it to a depth of three feet. Then he worked three layers of manure into the soil, topping it up with a final layer of fine soil brought from the bottom of the trench. Now the sowing trenches were made – three feet apart and six inches deep. Into these went leaf soil on top of the tubers with ample spacing between each tuber; and just to lend a welcome note of variety to the crop, Fred planted twelve different sorts of potato. Before they were given their first earthing up, the ground was covered with a thick layer of newly mown grass – and as the crop began to flourish Fred had the satisfaction of seeing that here was the promise of one of the best potato harvests he had ever produced. In fact those potatoes yielded twenty-four tons to the acre – and the workmen had the grace to admit that Fred had made the impossible come true.

"My next little caper," Fred remembered "was at the Dublin Show. Now most of the exhibitors in those days were the big nurserymen who'd got no end of money to spend and no end of time licking their exhibits into shape. So I decided I'd let them see how things were done in London!"

Working solidly through the night before opening day, Fred created in the centre of the Show Hall a breathtakingly realistic woodland scene. Somehow he contrived to introduce a shy little stream into the glade, with moss covered stones and a nearby group of wood lilies. This was one occasion when Fred, the skilled flower arranger, forgot all about formality. His aim was to lure the visitor right away from the noise and bustle of Dublin and deep into the springtime freshness of the woods. His rustic scene did just that.

A few minutes before the Show was due to open, Fred put the final touches to his masterpiece. Those were the days when exhibits carried no cards to reveal their origins, so as Fred made his way quietly to the washroom, debate and discussion in the Exhibition Hall was quickly into its stride. Whose hand had been at work to such stunningly good purpose? Whose particular brand of magic was this?

Some said this was an extravagant advertising stunt mounted by one of the biggest nurseries intent on outshining their rivals. Others believed this was a municipal exhibit, designed to show off the talents of the local parkkeepers. In any event, the woodland scene was awarded a Gold Medal and though Straffan had been savagely criticised for employing an English gardener, there were now plenty of congratulatory handshakes for the man who could win a 'Gold' against the best of the Irish. 'The Luck of the English' observed one of his rivals without a hint of malice.

"Yet I had to admit it Frank," said Fred, "my happiest days in Ireland were over now. Every month the troubles got worse. One night we'd hear of a railway line being wrecked nearby; next night it would be a drill hall burned down or a signal box destroyed. There was no peace in that lovely country. Not that I could really blame them for acting like that. I'd fought for my country. Now they felt they were fighting for theirs. But one thing I did know – it was none of my business."

Five years after his post-war return to Ireland, Fred said a final farewell to Straffan with many regrets but with genuine relief as well. And though the next three years brought two brief spells at Broxbourne in Hertfordshire and nearby at Wall Hall, Aldenham, Fred had to wait until the early months of 1926 for what he always described as 'the most exciting letter I ever received'.

The envelope that dropped through his letter-box bore an impressive crest and the postmark 'Petworth'. It contained a letter from Lord Leconfield telling Fred that the post of Head Gardener at Petworth House had fallen vacant and enquiring if he wished to be considered for the position. If so, he should present himself to the Agent at the Petworth Estate Office at ten o'clock sharp the following Thursday morning.

The letter said little more – apart from suggesting that he might care to spend the night at the Swan Hotel in Petworth to be sure of being on time for his appointment. Yet as Fred was to learn, both the style of the letter and its emphasis on promptness were typical of its writer, Lord Leconfield. He was a man whose distaste of verbosity was matched only by his dislike of unpunctuality.

"Ten o'clock sharp," Fred remembered, "and I was tapping on that Estate Office door. 'Come in' says a voice . . . and there I was having my first glimpse of Mr. Watson the Agent. The nicest man you could wish to meet, and right from the start I somehow felt at home there."

Fred had good reason to feel at home. His birthplace at Pulborough was no more than five miles down the road. Lavington Park (with its *pince-nez* agent and its memories of meagre pay rises) lay a few miles in the other direction towards Chichester. Still another link with Petworth was discovered during that first conversation with Lord Leconfield, for Fred learnt to his surprise that his mother's parents had been tenant farmers on the Leconfield Estate long before he was born.

"Mark you," Fred admitted "I was very careful what I said in that interview because I'd been warned that his Lordship could be a bit touchy – and a word out of place might easily spoil my chances. So I was just a bit relieved when he said – 'Well Streeter I've said all I want to say. Now I'll get Mr. Watson to show you round. Come back and have another word with me when you're finished.'"

Fred was never a man to bridle at the sheer magnitude of a job. He was far more likely to give voice to one of his exclamatory "Cooors . . ." when being told that the first primrose of Spring had been sighted than on learning that hundreds of acres of woodlands and parks and orchards were now to be entrusted to his care – not to mention a pair of lakes and a small township of glasshouses. All these – and more – were to be Fred's province should he decide to accept the Petworth job. He made up his mind very quickly. Walking briskly back to the Estate Office with Mr. Watson, Fred felt a strange exhilaration at what he had seen, and what now lay ahead of him. If you can ring a door bell jauntily that's just what he did as he arrived at the office door.

"Well?" enquired the word-sparing Lord Leconfield. "Interested?" "Yes, my Lord. With your permission I'll take the job," Fred replied.

"Very good. Draw your expenses from my secretary and arrange with Mr. Watson when you'll start: And now good day to you Streeter!''

That was all. No formal signing of documents to confirm that one of Britain's proudest estates had now come under his care. No charging of glasses with the likeable Mr. Watson to celebrate their new partnership. Only a word of warning that his Lordship was not exactly wedded to change and that since, in the last hundred years, there had only been three Head Gardeners at Petworth, Fred Streeter should introduce any innovations he had in mind both with tact and with caution.

Fred heeded those words. But as he journeyed back to break the good news to Hilda, he had already decided he would imprint something of his own personality on Petworth Park – and if his gardens didn't become some of the finest gardens in the land, then his name was not Frederick Streeter.

March 25th 1926 was a brilliantly sunny day at Petworth. It was also the day of Fred's arrival as Head Gardener, and he took it as a happy omen that his favourite flower, the primrose, was already flowering at the roadside as he made his way towards the gates.

Hilda had decided that she would join him a few days later, giving him a chance to get the measure of his duties. But before he got down to work, he decided to request a further brief interview with Lord Leconfield. He could not fully enjoy his work here until his status had been firmly established – and although many might say he was working in the shadow of the legendary 'Capability Brown', Fred knew full well that the only successful gardener is the one who stands squarely on his own two feet.

"If I am to do really well here Sir," said Fred to his Lordship "I must be given a free hand."

"A free hand; does that mean you think you're better than Capability Brown?" came the mildly reproachful reply.

"Well of course," said Fred, "he had all the help and all

the facilities he wanted. Give me the same and I reckon I could take him on."

Many specialists in the world of landscape gardening have since drawn comparisons between the two men . . . the man who could see 'great capability' in almost every swell and curve of land and the calmer, quieter Fred who could create a floral symphony within the confines of a single flowerbed.

Brown conceived his designs in the grand manner and his early work at Petworth shows how he expressed himself with a spectacular disregard for time and money. He had a stream dammed to create a lake. He proposed a whole succession of new buildings including a sumptuous orangery. He swept away a delightful formal garden which was too pedantic in concept to suit his master plan. And, if the old records are to be believed, in a single edict he passed the death sentence on a bowling green, a greenhouse and even a small banqueting house in the woods – presumably insisting that he could see 'little capability' in them.

Fred's approach to the re-design of a garden was of a less revolutionary kind. He would distill a wealth of skill and imagination into a once humble herbaceous border; he would plan a flowerbed not only for its shape and style (promising that every plant would have a chance to display its wonders), but would so order the bed that it promised a succession of colours right through the changing seasons.

On the one occasion I asked Fred for his views on his distinguished and 'capable' predecessor, he simply replied – "Well of course I never knew him Frank. He finished gardening about a hundred years before I started."

Soon after his arrival at Petworth, Fred Streeter had his first meeting with the Lady of the House, Lady Leconfield. The encounter was friendly to the point of informality.

"There are one or two things," she said, "that I feel you should know about my husband."

Fred was tempted to observe that he had already formed

one or two opinions of his own; but he merely nodded, said nothing and waited.

"He's an absolute stickler for punctuality," she continued hoping no doubt to smooth the path for her new Head Gardener. "If he tells you to report to him at ten o'clock, be sure to tap on his study door just as the last note is striking. Otherwise he'll insist that you're either too early or too late."

"I follow ma'am," Fred replied, realising that some of the stories he'd heard about his employer were almost certainly well founded.

"And for goodness sake," her Ladyship continued, "Never be tempted to ask him how he feels – or he'll tell you that he pays you to look after his gardens, not his health."

Lady Leconfield looked at him searchingly and Fred realised that her catalogue of warnings was not yet quite complete.

"One final point. Don't be tempted to be too talkative, Mr. Streeter. The first time we had a new barber visit us here the poor man enquired very politely – 'How does your Lordship like his hair cut?' I'm afraid my husband simply replied – 'In silence!'"

Fred was grateful for these well-meant warnings and decided that in Lady Leconfield he had a kindly ally. Yet he soon detected that a bond of confidence, growing encouragingly near to friendship, was also developing with Lord Leconfield. His Lordship had confessed, for example, that he couldn't stand sightseers peering over the walls when he took his strolls across the Petworth lawns. His previous Head Gardener had made some extravagant promises by way of a cure for this but somehow those promises had never materialised. He therefore warmed to the decisive way Fred solved the problem; he would plant a large yew hedge fully six feet high which would take a few years to establish itself but would eventually be so thick and unyielding that scarcely a mouse could penetrate.

"Now perhaps you can hardly credit this Frank," said Fred, "but I was no fool in those days and I always remembered the advice that one old gardener had given me about the way to get on with a new boss. Don't lay down the law to him right at the start; don't say you're going to do this and do that in the first few months you're there. No . . . let *him* do the talking and just chip in occasionally with an idea or two of your own. That way he'll be convinced he thought of it first – and you'll get your own way without any upsets."

So it was at Petworth. Fred set out to make friends with everyone, not only in the higher echelons of Lords and Ladies but with the staff as well; and one of his first friends was the cook.

"What lovely copper you have here," he observed to her, glancing round her kitchen at the glowing ranks of burnished copper pans. "And how beautifully you keep them."

This was music to the good cook's ears.

"Now what I'd like to know is whether you're getting all the fruit and vegetables you need" Fred continued. "Come to think of it, is there anything *new* in the vegetable line you'd particularly like in the kitchen, because I know how you ladies love preparing new dishes."

In those brief moments of verbal balm Fred established a bond of friendship that endured for years. Almost overwhelmed by such overtures the cook replied – "It's very kind of you to enquire so nicely Mr. Streeter. I'm sure we shall get on splendidly together."

So they did – and steadily the cook began to notice that a growing variety of fruits was arriving in the kitchen for bottling and preserving. Not just the predictable raspberries and gooseberries, pears and apples; but peaches and nectarines of new magnificence; quinces for that subtly flavoursome jelly; cranberries of such size and succulence that the good cook could scarcely believe her eyes; and such a profusion of red and white currants that she began to wonder how the arrival of one small man had breathed such gusts of vitality through the gardens.

Meantime, Lady Leconfield was taking daily stock of her blossoming flower gardens and finding growing pleasure in what she saw. It was rich now with an abundance of golden lilies and delphiniums, petunias and roses and salvias. This man, she told herself, not only knew how to make things grow; he had an eye for style and colour too. Perhaps these talents could now be turned to the benefit of Petworth House itself, which in its stately halls and galleries was somehow lacking in colour.

"We started our tour of the House, her Ladyship and I, in her own little sitting room," Fred recalled. "It was a long and narrow room Frank but it had some lovely views across the lawns and over to the Park as well."

"I love flowers," Lady Leconfield told Fred, "But I can never seem to get enough of them. So as we go round the house, why not tell me what you suggest we should have – the sort of flowers that will show off each room to best advantage."

"It was quite an eye-opener Frank. I'd been in some biggish places before but never anything quite like this. And when we came to the lovely marble hall – Cooor what a place that was to decorate. Her Ladyship wanted plants that reached right up to the ceiling – but she said 'Whatever you do, don't let your men spill any water on the floor – it's marble you know and it's treated once a week. So I want you to be extra careful'."

Quite a challenge that was – and more was to come. For as they made their way together down the main staircase, Lady Leconfield remarked that here she would like to see a massive six-foot vase with flowers cascading from it, just to set off the grandeur of the staircase to best advantage.

"But," she warned, pointing to the carpet. "This carpet is a masterpiece. *Never* let your men step on it!"

"So you see," Fred recalled, "that's where I learned

another lesson. How to put really large floral displays in position without damaging the floors or the furniture. Not like some folk I could mention . . . even some of the ladies I'm afraid. There are splashes of water everywhere and there's pollen and petals and goodness knows what all over the place. That's not the way to do it. Flowers are delicate things and if you handle them delicately they'll behave themselves splendidly. Just like well trained children you know!"

Now it could be said in fairness that the behaviour pattern of children was something of which Fred knew little; for although these were early days at Petworth, he had already been married for twenty-one years and still no family had arrived.

"I never really had time for *that* sort of thing," Fred insisted. "And to tell the truth it didn't worry me that we had no 'cuttings'. They might have crawled all over my flower beds or damaged my seedlings! No, I was a gardener Frank — and that was the end of it."

Meanwhile in the gardens of Petworth Fred's sphere of influence grew wider with every month that passed. Right from the start, he had been unhappy at the state of the kitchen garden — all seven acres of it! Earlier gardeners had reaped generations of splendid crops here, but now it wore the woeful look of soil that had lost all heart.

Fred set his men the task of digging it out. Down and down they went, three or four feet deep, to find that the ground was packed with rubbish and rubble which told its own little history of honest toil. Bricks and twisted metalwork — even rotting spades and forks abandoned perhaps by long dead gardeners. All this was removed and scrapped, to be replaced by a rich layer of manure right at the bottom of the trench — and further dressings of manure worked into the soil as the level was gradually re-established. Here, in effect, Fred Streeter created a brand new kitchen garden on the site of the old. It was a long task and some might say a more superficial approach would have yielded much the same dividends. But Fred wouldn't agree. He was no advocate of deep digging for deep digging's sake, but when it was the surest way to blend new nourishment into the soil, then he would dig along with the best of them!

"Let's admit it Frank," Fred would say, "there are some vegetables like carrots for instance that aren't all that keen on well manured soil. But most crops are pretty heavy feeders. Onions for instance; they'll go rooting down for manure that's deep in the soil. And potatoes too – they'll say 'thank you' for plenty of compost. Even the dear old cabbage puts on a far better show if he's rewarded with a lovely dressing of manure."

No wonder that noble visitors to Petworth between the wars began to relish their stay at the Big House, not merely for the delights of the company there but for the delectable vegetables that were brought to table. All of which pleased Lady Leconfield especially, for although she had a finely tuned palate and an appreciative eye for well grown garden produce, her own efforts at gardening were ill starred. She had admitted this to Fred Streeter within days of his arrival at Petworth.

"Everything I sow simply doesn't come up . . . and everything I plant seems to die in a day or so. What do you suppose I'm doing wrong?"

Fred felt a pang of sympathy for her and nodded towards the church nearby.

"Now you see that spire your Ladyship. If for some reason you wanted it pulled down, you wouldn't dream of doing it yourself would you? You'd ask someone like me to get it done for you. Well it's just the same with your seeds and plants. I'm here to take care of them. When you want something done in the garden, just send for me."

Lady Leconfield liked that little parable. She said so to Fred – adding "And now, Mr. Streeter, I think we understand one another perfectly!"

It was some months after this meeting that Lady Lecon-field dared to mention the little matter of the sunken garden. Not such a little matter at that! Ever since child-hood she had dreamed of having a sunken garden as a pri-vate retreat from the world. Perhaps it was somehow linked with the fact that most children love playing hide-and-seek, and the mere thought of being able to hide in a sunken garden had always appealed to her.

"I suggest," said Fred, on hearing her wishes, "That the best place for your sunken garden would be where the aspa-ragus is planted now."

Even to the resilient Lady Leconfield, this suggestion came as something of a surprise. Those asparagus beds had been the pride of Petworth for close on half a century. Yet Fred convinced her that asparagus is an adaptable crop and that anyhow it might well be time for a change of bed. So soon the move was made and Fred had a team of men busy digging the site to a depth of six feet.

"Some of those men," Fred admitted, "began to think that they were miners instead of gardeners. No sooner had they finished all that trenching in the kitchen garden than here they were, busy at work on her Ladyship's sunken garden. But what a lovely job they made of it."

In the centre of the sunken garden Fred decided to have a lily pond, complete with fountain. A flagged pathway led from the pool towards the steps giving access to the sunken garden, while around its perimeter a wall was built of stone and moss and rockery plants. Within the sheltered confines of the garden, Fred spread himself in a prodigal burst of colour. Two thousand plants he selected – and to this day the sense of peace he created here still lingers on.

To fashion a sunken garden in the vintage Streeter manner, you need not only space and light but a sur-rounding landscape of generous proportions. Fred was once asked, however, about the possibilities of a sunken garden in a smaller setting; his answer was that many modest suburban gardens could benefit if only the man in charge would think occasionally of digging *down* rather than always turning his hopeful eyes to Heaven!

From hot house to sunken garden . . . from the making of a mulberry walk to the tending of the finest cranberry beds in Britain. Sometimes it seemed that Petworth's demands on the time and talents of Fred Streeter would never come to an end.

"Mark you," Fred admitted to me, "I really revelled in all that responsibility, because some of the most important people in the land came down to Petworth. And once they'd paid us a visit they came to realise that our gardens were something extra special."

When Fred arrived at Petworth he had thirty-five men under his immediate control, and he quickly formed the impression that few of them knew how to fill their time productively.

"Trouble with them, like so many so-called gardeners Frank, was that they wouldn't stick to one task at a time. They'd keep shifting around from one spot to another, never really completing the job they'd set out to do. So here's a tip for any gardener. Decide on the little plot of land you're going to work on this morning or this afternoon. Size it up carefully so you're sure you can cope with it – and then don't dare touch anything else until that first job is finished!"

Some members of Fred's team had been working at Petworth for thirty or forty years when he arrived; it took courage as well as tact to introduce them to new ways.

"As a matter of fact," said Fred, "one old fellow called Eli had been there for sixty years and there were stories that he was a rather touchy old devil. One of the men warned me – 'Don't you upset old Eli will you Mr. Streeter?' Well I replied, I don't want to upset anyone, but if I'm not happy with what old Eli's up to, I'll have to tell him off – just like anyone else!"

Soon after this exchange Eli changed jobs for the first time in sixty years! As to the reasons for his going, Fred remained tactfully silent. The plain truth was that many a man not directly employed by the Estate saw Petworth House as a handy meal ticket in those days – and if the popular conception of Fred Streeter was a man of unfailingly gentle character who travelled benevolently through life, the Fred of those revolutionary days at Petworth was very different.

"It's like feeding a blinking factory," the foreman of the kitchen garden complained to him. "It's not just the folk in the dining room and the stewards' room and the servants' hall and the pantry. It's all the outsiders as well!"

Fred had planned from the start to make friends with everyone who came within this particular orbit, but he had certainly no intention of providing a ready-made benevolent society for the 'outsiders'.

"Right then," he said decisively. "From now on nothing leaves the gardens without orders from Lord or Lady Leconfield – or from me. Understand?"

Everyone understood – and from that day on, two significant changes were to be detected at Petworth. The 'outsiders' melted away, disenchanted by the realisation that their wheedling ways would cut no ice with Fred Streeter; while Fred discovered (not without some regret) that less and less of his time was being spent in the gardens while more and more hours would find him in his office, checking the garden accounts or deploying his team for tomorrow's work.

More than this: Fred realised that here at Petworth he was even expected to be something of an historian, and whenever the gardens were open to the public and enquiring visitors surged in, he became a target for their questions. He therefore armed himself with a working knowledge of the history of Petworth House and a ready turn of phrase for almost every enquiry that came his way, even if some of those enquiries seemed singularly pointless.

"I think the worst thing any onlooker can ask a gardener," said Fred, "is simply – 'What are you doing *there?*' Makes him feel as though he's up to no good Frank – as if he shouldn't be there in the first place. So I used to say to my men – "If anyone asks you what you're doing, tell 'em you could do with a hand and offer them a spade. They'll push off quick enough then!"

When King George V was convalescing from a near fatal illness at nearby Bognor, Queen Mary was a regular visitor to Petworth. She would be driven over to Petworth through villages with rural, rugged names like Eartham and Duncton and Funtington – delighting on the journey to see the noble company of elms and oaks and chestnuts that stood guard along the peaceful lanes of Sussex.

Arriving at Petworth, the Queen would walk quietly in the gardens with one of her ladies-in-waiting. It was on just such a visit that she happened to peep into a hothouse to find Fred Streeter intent on the task of spraying with soft water a newly flowering family of blooms – a task he would entrust to no one else. The Queen had heard already that Fred was particularly proud of his orchids and she was anxious to know how they were progressing. But more than that . . . she wanted to solve another little mystery.

"Is it really true," she enquired of Fred, "that you actually talk to your flowers?" She had heard it rumoured, but she could scarcely credit that it was so.

"Perfectly true ma'am," Fred assured her. "I talk to them just like I talk to any other friends. And if one of them looks a bit sorry for himself I simply say – 'Come on old chap, cheer up. Shall I fetch you a drink?' It works wonders you know ma'am, because plants have feelings just like the rest of us."

Fred turned at this point to show the Queen a batch of cuttings that were prospering near by.

"Now take those cuttings ma'am," he continued, "when

92

I first put them into that rooting medium, they looked just like little lost souls. In fact I was afraid I was going to lose the lot. But I said to them one morning – 'Do you remember who your father was . . . he was a fine great plant and I want you all to grow up nice and strong so you'll be a credit to him.' And after that they rooted away splendidly and they've never looked back."

The Queen nodded gravely. "I must remember that," she said. And then with a regal smile she added – "And how are the *latest* additions to your family Mr. Streeter?"

Just for a moment Fred was lost for words. Then he realised what the Queen meant. She was enquiring about his newest batch of seedlings! So deeper into the greenhouse went the Queen and the gardener to discover how Petworth's latest arrivals were progressing.

On another occasion, Queen Mary questioned Fred in depth about the qualities which, to his mind, went to the making of a really successful Head Gardener.

Fred smiled as he recalled the conversation. "I don't know whether she wasn't all that satisfied with the chap she had up at Buckingham Palace at the time Frank – and I didn't like to ask her in case she thought I was after his job!"

"So what did you tell her Fred?" I enquired.

"Well I simply said that I reckoned he needed about thirty years experience, coming up through the ranks as it were, before he took over as Head Gardener. Otherwise he might be one of these bright young chaps who thinks he knows it all just because he's read all the right gardening books!"

"Does that mean Fred," I asked, "that you've really not much time for book-learning as far as gardening is concerned?"

Fred paused a moment before he replied – "Well put it this way Frank. You won't catch me out on the names – the *proper* names – of anything you can find in the garden. In

93

my time I've spent hundreds of hours with my head in books, and thousands of hours studying the seed catalogues. But books can only start you off on the right path. After that, it's up to you!"

I sometimes wondered how Queen Mary reacted to Fred's advice about choosing a Head Gardener and whether she ever put it into practice. Whatever the answer, this much is certain. Queen Mary was far from being the only Royal visitor to Petworth who would quietly seek advice from Fred.

"One chap," Fred recalled, "came all the way from Japan to pay me a visit. The Crown Prince of Japan I believe Frank, and his Dad sent him over to me to learn about flower arranging."

Now it had always been my firm conviction that if there was one art in which the Japanese reigned supreme, it was surely the art of flower arrangement. The way they can coax a wealth of eloquence from a single bloom has never failed to intrigue me. So – with all due deference to Fred Streeter – I couldn't help wondering why a young Prince should travel nearly half way round the world to study flower arrangement at Petworth.

"Aaaah," said Fred, relishing the opportunity I'd set up for him. "It was like this Frank. His father had been here at Petworth years ago and had kept in touch ever since. So he knew I was a bit of a dab hand at flower arranging, specially at all those parties and banquets we had. That's why he wanted his boy to come over to learn the English way with flowers."

The Crown Prince and his tutor remained for three months in Petworth, staying at The Swan Hotel in the heart of the town. But then the clouds of war had rolled across the horizon and Prince and tutor had hurried back home. Yet as a pleasant post-script to their visit they had sent Fred three small magnolia trees which still flourish to this day at Petworth.

"Seemed to me Frank," said Fred "that no sooner had we forgotten about one war than another bit of bother started brewing up. But of course I was so busy in those days that I scarcely had time to worry about what that chap Hitler was up to!"

But Fred was too busy to pay much attention to Hitler. Many of his plans for the gardens had now come to fruition; in particular, the 'reconditioned' kitchen garden was day by day providing a veritable feast of vegetables. It needed to, for scarcely a week-end would pass without a lavish house party being staged at Petworth.

"Early in the morning I'd be nipping into the kitchen to make sure that the cook had everything she needed – then into the House itself to see about the decorations. If it was summer of course I'd rely a lot on cut flowers for decoration. But in the winter – well that was the time when the pot plants came into their own."

Fred had a place in his designs for all the conventional house plants – the azaleas and cyclamen; the extravagantly named *Saint-paulia Ionantha* or African Violet. But his special gift was that he could produce an indoor riot of colour every week of the year, yet never once would his displays repeat themselves.

Fred indeed was a man for all seasons; and at an age when many are planning a prudent slackening of the working pace, Fred in his late fifties was leading a more crowded life than ever. Had he known of the added demands that broadcasting was soon to make on him, perhaps he would have declined C. H. Middleton's invitation to take part in that first programme on that memorable Sunday afternoon in 1935.

Yet once he had taken those first steps to Portland Place, there was no turning back. He was the architect of his own future and the success of his first broadcast was so immediate that, even before he left Broadcasting House, he had unknowingly committed himself to a new and demanding career.

The Producer was full of praise, saying that Fred had brought a refreshing zest to the programme. His advice had doubtless given listeners a new enthusiasm for growing runner beans; and as for his suggestion that we should sow our peas at least a foot apart . . . well that would bring a torrent of critical correspondence from suburban gardeners. Never mind; a little controversy was the lifeblood of a programme such as this.

But there was just one thing . . . "Next time," warned the Producer, "don't say so much in a single broadcast. Keep more up your sleeve Mr. Streeter. Otherwise you'll soon run out of subjects and that would never do!"

That Sunday evening when Fred returned to Petworth, his critics were waiting for him. Hilda Streeter said he'd been splendid on the wireless but did he really have to drop every single 'h'? Lady Leconfield had loved to hear his rich Sussex tones rolling out over the air; but did he really have quite such a deep voice as that?

Lord Leconfield alone was unstinting in his praise. He looked solemnly at the newly famous Fred Streeter and observed – "Only the aristocracy knows me Streeter. But after today the world knows you."

VII

"Every now and again cast your eyes round your garden and if you can spot a single patch that's not pulling its weight, start experimenting till you find just the right crop to suit those particular conditions. It'll probably take a bit of time and a lot of patience Frank, but it'll pay you in the end."

Fred could never be called a short-tempered man. But beware his wrath if anyone suggested that a particular garden or type of soil was good for nothing.

"Don't you believe it," he would sternly correct them, "there may be plenty of useless gardeners about and I've met plenty of them in my time. But there's no such thing as a useless garden. Let's suppose you've got a shaded patch in the garden where nothing seems to grow or a poor old stretch of soil that's been working hard for years; I'll bet you can still raise some lovely perpetual spinach there. It's a marvellous little crop you know and it can save you a small fortune in vegetable bills. Come to think of it, you can usually grow a nice row of carrots and even a few lettuce on poorish ground as well. So never let me hear you say that your soil is good for nothing."

Fred's talents at reaping maximum returns from the soil were soon to be given full rein during the 'dig for victory' years of the Second World War. Since his return from France in 1917, when a period of convalescence from his wounds had brought a spell of enforced rest, he had scarcely known a single day of relaxation.

Even when Lady Leconfield sensed he might benefit from a break and sent him to Paris on the agreeable mission of touring the notable gardens of the capital, he somehow could not settle at the comfortable little hotel in which she had booked him and soon he was making plans for an early return to Petworth.

"One look at that hotel menu Frank," he confessed, "and I knew I was sunk. I didn't want to find myself ordering snails or something – without knowing it. What a blessing I discovered that there was one waiter who could speak English. I got him to bring me a nice plateful of plain food instead of all that saucy stuff the French love – and we were friends for ever more."

Lady Leconfield had even arranged that Fred should visit the Baron Rothschild at his home off the Champs Elysées – so that the Baron might advise him in more detail about the gardens he should inspect. As it happened, Baron Rothschild was convinced that Paris had far greater attractions to offer Fred than mere gardens – and was soon insisting that his man would accompany Fred that night to the Folies Bergères and to the glittering night-life of Montmartre. Fred was equally insistent that he had come to see the gardens – and while the Baron could not fathom such unswerving dedication to duty, at last he relented. Fred should see just as many gardens as he wished.

In fact, Fred's horticultural tour of the capital was

something of a disappointment. In the Chateau Malmaison he was unimpressed by the much vaunted rose gardens. At Versailles, the richness of the floral displays seemed blunted by the dust that was everywhere.

"Perhaps I'd chosen the wrong time of year for this visit," Fred admitted, "because I'm sure there are plenty of Frenchmen who are first-rate gardeners. But you know what they say . . . first impressions are always the ones that last. And that's the way it was on my visit to France."

True, on a tour of the Paris markets he was much impressed by the range of vegetables on display — and he applauded the French housewife for being far less conventional in her choice than her British counterpart. But he was also shocked when he saw the *size* of some of the vegetables being bought by the supposedly shrewd housewives of the City.

"They didn't seem to appreciate Frank that half the secret of really good vegetables — the sort of vegetables you're proud to·bring to table — is to pick them while they're young. That way you get a really tender, sweet tasting little delicacy instead of some horsy old thing that takes you a month of Sundays to eat. Another thing — by picking your vegetables young, you encourage the plant to grow more for you. Otherwise the poor old thing will say to himself — 'Well he doesn't seem to want what I've grown already, so why should I bother to grow any more?'"

Of course, as radio listeners soon came to realise — Fred's plants always had voices; slightly treble voices in the case of tender blossoms, deep resonant tones for sturdy chaps like pumpkins and marrows. He brought these vocal talents into play when describing the Rose Gardens of Paris.

"When I looked at those roses Frank I could almost have wept," he declared, "they hadn't been properly pruned in their lives I should think. If I could have spoken French, I'd have given those gardeners a piece of my mind; instead of which I simply said to those roses — 'Well next time you come on this earth, come to Petworth instead of Paris. You'll soon see what good old Sussex soil can do for you.' Only trouble was Frank, I'm not too sure that those poor little specimens could understand English!"

In a sense Fred seemed proud when telling me that he never had a *real* holiday in his life. Even when I hinted that it had been a bit hard on Hilda never to enjoy a complete change of scene, he dismissed the suggestion as he might have dismissed a troublesome fly which had settled on his arm.

"Get away Frank," he said with that famous Fred Streeter chuckle. "When a lady marries a gardener, she knows what's in store for her – a nice healthy life with plenty of free vegetables and a lovely bunch of flowers every now and again."

And that was that.

In any event, the coming of September 1939 put paid to any plans for a holiday, and the man whom the Army had written off as totally disabled in 1917 now moved into battle once again.

That Sunday morning – September 3rd 1939 – Fred had followed his usual practice of making a brief tour of the gardens to reassure himself that all was in order; then, in company with Hilda, he had walked the quarter-mile from their home in the grounds of Petworth Park to attend morning service in the Parish Church. It was here that he heard the news that war had been declared.

As he walked back to the cottage (though to describe his mid-Victorian house as a cottage always seemed rather misleading to me) there was a new urgency in his step. He had already enlisted in the Special Constabulary and had attended several lectures on map reading, first aid and so on. But now the rehearsals were over. This was the real thing. He told Hilda that Sunday dinner would have to wait, that she was to expect him when she saw him, and away he went to Petworth Police Station secretly admitting that today, for all his 62 years, there was something distinctly exciting in the air.

Scarcely had the sad voiced Neville Chamberlain broken the news of war than the air-raid sirens were telling an unbelieving nation that the Luftwaffe was on the way. Of course, it wasn't! Some off-course plane had given the war a false but flying start. But in Petworth, as in towns and villages right through the country, that first alarm had all the significance of a starting gun. The chips were down; the gun covers were off; and Fred Streeter was climbing into his uniform as Inspector of the Special Constabulary, Petworth Division.

Geographically speaking, Petworth could not wish for a finer setting. It stands high on a hill which falls away on the eastern edge of the town with a dramatic gradient towards Pulborough. Westward lie Midhurst and the Hampshire border. Nestling close to Petworth is the unassuming little village of Fittleworth which has among its claims to fame one of the most dangerous right-angle bends imaginable, aptly named Hallelujah Corner.

Petworth Park itself is massive territory. It is a land of deer parks and lakes and towering trees. The very gateway to Petworth House has its own spectacular feature for it is flanked by two giant stone pillars which dominate the centre of the village and watch over it with a wonderful sense of permanence. The landscape painter Turner knew and loved Petworth House and was a constant visitor here. He had his own studio in the House and a fine selection of his paintings are today displayed in the Turner Room. And then there are the walls of Petworth Park, stretching fourteen miles around those rolling acres. Much of this was Inspector Streeter's territory when, on the evening of Monday September 4th, he marched out of Petworth Police Station on his first tour of duty.

"Of course," Fred told me once, "that very spot on which the Police Station stands was once the site of old

Petworth Prison. And what a place that was! They say that the poor old prisoners spent most of their time on the tread-mill there, and the only food they ever got was bread and water. No wonder they dropped from exhaustion."

"Mark you," he went on, "There are all manner of stories to be told about Petworth. Saint Mary's Church here for instance used to have a pretty crooked old spire – very tall but very crooked. That's how we got the rhyme 'Proud Petworth, Poor People, High Church, Crooked Steeple!' "

Now although Fred had already been living in Petworth for thirteen years, so much of his time had been spent within the walls of Petworth Park that there had been surprisingly little opportunity for social contact in the town. He was not a man for pubs and clubs; on the contrary there were many in Petworth who thought of him as a stern, unbending man – a man to turn to in an hour of need rather than to seek for a merry evening's company.

Those early days of the war were strangely beautiful in this part of Sussex. The weather stayed hot and dry as summer refused to take a final bow. Late on those sultry evenings the people of Petworth would hear the occasional throb of a distant plane or would see, away towards the coast, a cone-shaped searchlight looping lazily over the sky. But if this was war, peace could scarcely be more tranquil.

Yet the first of War's minor revolutions had already made its strident impact on the peace of this little town. And the particular impact that broke upon the Streeters late one golden afternoon in early September had come from the improbable source of Peckham Rye.

Joan and Thelma Hewitt, two very small and timid girls aged nine and six were evacuated from London and came to stay with the Streeters. When they arrived at their destination, they found that Mrs. Streeter (a name they felt they could trust) was not at home. The gentleman who met them at the door was kindly, it is true, but seemed distant to the point of being ill-at-ease – even as if he had been secretly hoping that they hadn't been coming in the first place.

"Did you have a nice journey?" Fred asked them hopefully. The two children said not a word.

"How about something to eat?" Fred enquired. In unison Joan and Thelma sadly shook their heads.

Fred called Hilda's dog Teddy (a little brown pom) to the rescue; but the dog came leaping into the kitchen with such enthusiasm that the children retreated into a corner while Fred was already beginning to wonder whether it might be possible to swap Joan and Thelma for two rather more talkative boys.

At that moment he heard with relief the crunch of Hilda's feet on the gravel driveway – and in seconds the capable Mrs. Streeter (with hours of schoolroom experience to her credit) had brought a smile to Thelma's face and a positive torrent of information from Joan.

Their Mum, she learned, had a wartime office job now. Dad was too old for the Army and was working in a big hotel. Then there was a married sister and two brothers as well. As for the happenings of today, the two of them hadn't really known they were coming to stay here until this very morning though they suspected Mum and Dad knew about it all along – but didn't tell them in case they couldn't sleep and were sick in the night.

"Those children settled down beautifully," Fred recalled. "After a while they'd even give me a hand in the garden from time to time. And that's where things were beginning to get difficult, because it wasn't long before some of my chaps were being called up and we had to make all manner of changes."

Fred knew full well that these changes were necessary. He recognised that the flower borders must go, to give place to vegetables. He knew that the greenhouse boilers could no longer indulge their voracious appetites on those weekly tons of coke. And when he heard that most of the rooms in Petworth House were to be closed for the duration, he knew that those golden days of banquets and parties and laughter on the lawns were probably gone for ever. Yet strangely enough there were some compensations.

Promotion in the Specials had already come Fred's way. He was now a Superintendent and with this promotion came a growing call on his services. Scarcely a week would pass without some directive from H.Q. in the early hours of the morning to seek out a supposedly unexploded bomb or to search the woods for an often suspected but never discovered German parachutist.

As happened in many villages in those days, the Specials came in for more than their share of criticism. So did the L.D.V., who later became the Home Guard. 'Playing at soldiers' some of the cynics would say – never quite certain what duties the Specials were fulfilling, but content to brush them aside as a pantomime version of the real thing.

The critics changed their tune one afternoon in 1942.

Just outside Petworth, in the rustically named Pheasants' Copse, was stationed a large contingent of Polish and Canadian troops. They had been greeted in Petworth with mixed feelings. Their late-night songs and their amorous adventures down the cobbled streets after closing time were not always to the liking of the older residents. Yet many said it was jolly good for a staid old place like Petworth to have an infusion of new blood wished upon it and the longer the troops stayed at Pheasants' Copse, the better!

There were many whose thoughts turned to Pheasants' Copse that day in 1942 when the sound of an aircraft engine throbbed uneasily over the town. Was that plane in trouble of some sort? Was it one of ours? If it wasn't – could it perhaps be seeking that troop concentration in Pheasants' Copse?

No one will ever know the answer. For in a sudden split second of awful devastation, the plane released one bomb which fell, not on Pheasants' Copse but on the village school. This was the Boys' Department of the school and, in that single moment, an unseen German airman left a scar on Petworth that could never completely heal.

Twenty-nine children and two schoolteachers died that day and now lie buried in the lower cemetery just on the northern outskirts of Petworth. Among the first to make his way into the smoking carnage was Fred Streeter. He had seen death and destruction on the horrific scale of Flanders. But the work he had to face that terrible afternoon was certainly the most heartbreaking task to which he ever set his hand.

Just as he was reluctant to speak of his bayonet wounds in France, so he was reticent to tell me much about the bombing of the village school. Yet the people of Petworth who can still recall the event will speak with reverence of the work of the Specials that day – helped by the Canadians from Pheasants' Copse. Still to this day, on the anniversary of the bombing, wreaths and flowers are piled high on the multiple grave in the lower cemetery; and among those who remember is Florrie Hallett (later to become Fred's companion), for she lost two younger brothers.

On a happier note, Joan and Thelma became firmer members of the family with every month that passed. Now they delighted to be taken for walks in the country; they talked unflatteringly little about Mum and Dad and Peckham Rye; Joan took on the job of delivering papers for the local newsagent; and both children relished the occasions when they could help Mrs. Streeter in such homely tasks as the making of blackcurrant jam or the slicing of runner beans to be preserved with layers of salt in sturdy brown preserving jars.

Thelma Hewitt (today still living in Peckham Rye) remembers a host of homely things about life with the Streeters in those wartime days. She remembers Hilda Streeter's skills in the making of wines – and the bottle upon bottle of elderberry and medlar wine stored in the cellar beneath the cottage. She remembers the variety of new vegetables and fruit to which the two young evacuees were introduced – the asparagus, the chicory and the piled-high bowls of strawberries and raspberries that always tasted so good because they came straight from the garden. She remembers Hilda's wonderful salads, made still more wonderful by a 'secret' ingredient, tarragon she suspected. And she remembers Mrs. Streeter's quite exceptional interest in birds – and those birds-nesting expeditions when Hilda would discover all manner of ornithological treasures yet never disturb a single egg.

"But the strange thing is," Thelma recalls, "that try as she might Mrs. Streeter could never really help me conquer my fear of cows! Joan and I became real country girls in almost every way. But – being a Londoner I suppose – I could never walk through those fields with Mrs. Streeter without looking over my shoulder to see whether the cows were after us! And as for Mr. Streeter of course – well he was a *real* character. He even taught us the right way to eat a peach – especially those lovely white English peaches he grew so well."

" 'You don't want to eat them all politely like some folk do' he would say. 'That's no good at all. Eat them just like you would an apple . . . and let the juice run right down your chin. That's the only way to enjoy the *real* flavour!' "

By this time of course Fred's team of workers at Petworth had diminished steadily until only half a dozen men remained. They laboured to good purpose producing such an abundance of fruit and vegetables that it was possible to send regular supplies to market. This was good for the war effort – and helpful to the dwindling exchequer of Petworth.

Visitors were still allowed in the gardens during part of the summer season and the entrance fee of one shilling did something to help one or two well chosen charities. But it wasn't all profit!

"I remember once," Fred said, "spotting a fat old lady

who was pulling peaches off the trees as fast as she could go, then stuffing them into a wicker basket affair. Course, she didn't know I was Head Gardener but I crept up beside her and suddenly said – 'What do you think you're up to, stealing all that fruit? Do you think you can take what you want just because you've paid a shilling?"

"Imagine my surprise Frank when instead of getting all flustered and starting to apologise she simply turned on me and said – 'Push off you old buffer' . . . then started pelting me with my own peaches. Cooor, what a nerve that woman had!"

It was now seven years or so since that first appearance on the air with C. H. Middleton; and although Fred was quick to correct me when I once suggested that this broadcast had made him a star overnight, his calls to Broadcasting House were growing steadily more and more frequent.

Wartime broadcasts with C. H. Middleton were usually on such stern matters as getting the most from an allotment – or explaining how the digging of heavy clay soil could be made a little easier for the lady of the house who was faced with this task while her husband was away at the wars.

More than this – Fred's emergence as a personality in his own right brought calls for talks and lectures to horticultural societies. Inevitably these talks were based on a 'dig for Victory' theme; and it was then perhaps that Fred developed his love for describing how even the miniature vegetable patch can prove "far better than money in the bank Frank. You never know what those financial fellows are going to do with the value of money. But the good old cabbage and the lettuce and the beetroot are always worth having!"

Around this time Fred was learning a lesson that comes to all new broadcasters; that the job isn't finished when the programme ends and the contributors leave the studio – elated or despondent according to how the broadcast has fared! Then come the listeners' letters. . . .

In my early days as an interviewer on television I received a letter which bore no address or signature but came in an envelope post-marked Portsmouth. It simply said: 'You have an uncanny knack for asking the wrong question to the wrong person at the wrong time.'

At first glance I felt a surge of fury that anyone should be so briefly bitter without even revealing their name; but on deeper study I had to admit that he (or she) had damned my career very neatly in the space of one short sentence.

Telling this particular story to Fred reminded him of some of his own early problems in this field.

"Of course," he recalled, "Old 'Middy' was a great one for having the right answer, no matter what the question might be. He had letters from listeners asking more or less everything under the sun; how to deal with warts and lumbago and corns – and even how to get rid of spiders in the pantry. But one of his best answers was to a chap who wanted some help with money matters. Old 'Middy' simply wrote back and said – 'Since I can't really manage my own financial affairs, I don't see that I can be much help with yours!' "

None the less when C. H. Middleton died on September 18th 1945 and Fred realised that the mantle of 'Radio Gardener' had now fallen firmly about his shoulders, the problem of sustaining two demanding careers had somehow to be faced – and solved. He was no longer a young man. On the contrary he would soon be in his seventies. But Fred had no time for people who judged their abilities by what the calendar said. After all, with the War now over, it seemed safe to assume that there would be no more nocturnal searches in the woods for lurking enemies and that some of the outdoor staff would soon be returning from the wars to lend a hand at Petworth.

"Those were lovely days on the wireless you know Frank," Fred told me. "I started to meet some wonderful

108

people like dear old Freddie Grisewood – and he soon had me on his 'Any Questions' programme. Then there was Ralph Wightman with that rich old Dorset voice of his. We did a programme called 'Country Magazine' together and – cooor, some of the tales old Ralph could tell. Not all of them fit for the wireless mind you!"

"While Middy was still alive we'd do several programmes together quite apart from his 'In your Garden' lark. But as soon as he died I began to realise that I'd have to get myself a bit more organised. Because where the gardeners had sent most of their queries to him – now, of course, they were coming to me instead."

Although the War had ended, most of Fred's correspondence still sounded a note of stern austerity. Some listeners would write complaining that, though food was still short and there were ration books in every handbag, the neighbours had started growing flowers again. Surely this shouldn't be allowed. We still needed all the vegetables we could grow . . . and it was Fred's duty to remind the country's gardeners of their responsibilities!

By now Fred's daily mailbag had reached such large proportions that the B.B.C. decided there was only one reasonable course of action. They would allow him the services of a secretary and he could dictate his letters to her, either after his broadcasts or whenever he cared to make a special visit to London.

"Well what a caper that was," Fred chuckled. "She was a nice enough girl mind you – and she wanted to be just as helpful as she could. So after one of my broadcasts I went down to this office they'd set aside for me and I gathered up all the letters I had to answer. Then in came this little secretary girl."

"She sat down opposite me, took out her pen and her shorthand notebook and said – 'Right Mr. Streeter, I'm ready'. Do you know Frank my mind seemed to go a blank. I was all right when I had a pen and paper of my own and could think out my answers carefully. But as for this business of dictating letters . . . cooor, that wasn't for me! Poor little girl, she looked quite upset. After I'd tried to answer a letter or two I had to tell her that it was very kind of her but I'd better go back to my old way of doing things. And that was that!"

In the matter of giving gardening advice on the radio, Fred observed one inflexible rule. He would never recommend a variety that he hadn't tested himself at first-hand; nor would he advise a method or technique with which he wasn't completely familiar. He firmly believed that successful gardening is a strictly co-operative effort, which explains why he found such huge satisfaction in sharing his ideas and inspirations with the millions who listened to him each week.

"After all," he'd say, "we gardeners are pretty friendly chaps . . . most of us anyhow! So why shouldn't we all benefit from one another's little triumphs? For instance, when you move to a new garden don't say to yourself – 'I'm going to show the chap next door a thing or two!' No . . . that's not the way at all! You want to lean over the garden fence and say – 'What varieties do best in this soil old man? I'm new to these parts and I want to learn.' That way he'll know you're a friendly sort of cove and the two of you will get on like a house on fire."

It is true of course that Fred had little first-hand experience of the 'back garden' brand of growing. The only small garden he had known intimately was that first childhood plot at Pulborough. And when he ultimately moved to Petworth he was following in the steps of the mighty – the gardener who worked in the grand manner.

An intriguing little note in the Guide Book to Petworth House says that 'Capability Brown's most characteristic contribution to the landscape at Petworth was the serpentine lake, enlarged from a small pond by judicious damming. The incomparable view this gave from the main front

110

of the house was later to inspire some of Turner's most elegiac landscapes, with the deer silhouetted against the setting sun. Little of this has changed since that day'.

Capability Brown's days at Petworth spanned the 1750's. Two hundred years later millions who had never heard of Capability Brown began to look on Fred Streeter as a friend. Not only had they heard him regularly on the wireless; he was in increasing demand to open fêtes and flower shows and even to lend his name to certain garden products. But though Fred never sought nor desired direct comparison with "that Capability fellow", comparisons were inevitably made. Most agreed that both men belonged to the noble company of "great gardeners". One far-seeing writer observed with some weight – "Fred may lack Brown's sweeping eye for landscape's most grandiloquent expressions; but it is equally probable that Brown lacked Fred's way with individual flower beds and his delicate touch with espaliered fruit. He actually talks to his flowers."

This was praise indeed to be awarded one or two marks ahead of Capability Brown. But praise had now come to Fred in a somewhat more tangible form. He had been recommended for the Victoria Medal of Honour, the highest tribute that the Royal Horticultural Society can bestow. Never had he made any conscious effort to fall in line for such an accolade; and though his triumphs in a positive succession of Shows had proved that here was a gardener of no ordinary ilk, the plain truth was that Fred had greatness thrust upon him.

He had never sought limelight in the Horticultural Halls of Fame, any more than he had tapped on the doors of Broadcasting House and asked – 'may I broadcast?'. He had quietly gone about the job he felt he was best fitted to fulfil, and fame had come scurrying in his footsteps.

And now it was television that beckoned him! The same routine of initial diffidence and of ultimate success . . .

111

"When they asked me first about going on the screen Frank I said 'Not on your life! A white-haired old codger like me? You can't be serious. I'd frighten off all your viewers!' " Yet a few days later Fred was busy rehearsing at Alexandra Palace, and new stardom was on the way!

British television had been on ice since close-down in September 1939. The service did not re-open until June 1946 and even then transmissions were restricted to the Crystal Palace Station. As late as 1949 Britain was still the only country to boast a complete television service and at the end of that year the world's most powerful television transmitting station came on the air at Sutton Coldfield.

The B.B.C. was negotiating now to take over film studios at Shepherds Bush but the centre of activity remained at Alexandra Palace. It was in the grounds of Ally Pally that Britain's first television garden plot came into being.

Fred described his first television rehearsal as something of an ordeal, not because he was nervous at the prospect of facing the cameras, but more that he had scarcely expected such a crowd of onlookers to be present for the occasion. Television in those days still had the heady tang of novelty and – learning that a well-known radio personality was about to be launched on the screen – a crowd had gathered to discover what the legendary Fred Streeter really looked like.

"Tell you the truth," Fred admitted to me, "I began to feel a bit like one of those blinking film stars myself. Everybody jostling around the fence that they'd set up to protect this little television garden and already one or two people asking if they could have my autograph. What a carry on! Course, that's the big difference between the wireless and the television. You can be on the wireless for years and apart from the occasional picture in the newspapers or in the 'Radio Times', nobody has the foggiest idea who you are. But a couple of minutes on that blessed television screen – and everybody's saying 'Well I'm blowed . . .

112

who'd have thought the old fellow looked like that.'"

In fact, the 'old fellow' put on a superb show for his introduction to television. He dealt that day with the planting out of geraniums and fuchsias, and once he'd learned the knack of regarding the camera as the all-seeing eye and resisting the temptation to mask his work with his own hands, the Producers up in the Control Room were wearing contented smiles and agreeing that gardening was a subject that would translate wonderfully to television.

It was now that Fred's own smile and his chuckle started on the road to fame. Viewers began to wait for those inimitable "Cooors" and "Aaaahs" which became just as much the Fred Streeter trademark as Jack Warner's "little gel" or Rob Wilton's "The day war broke out!"

It was at this stage too that the old Sussex gardener, now into his seventies, began to move into the glossy world of "show biz". He met – and was mentioned in the same breath as such personalities of the day as Philip Harben, the television cook; the irascible Gilbert Harding; Jeanne Heal who made her name in the fifties for her work on all manner of documentary programmes; and the announcers Winifred Shotter and Mary Malcolm who pioneered what many regard as the golden days of television as far as women were concerned.

In a copy of the Television Annual for 1953 I have spotted a delightful picture of Fred holding court in his Television Garden at Alexandra Palace. On the right are two elderly, stern-faced gentlemen described in the caption as 'horticultural specialists'. In the centre is the ever smiling Mary Malcolm. And – far left – is Fred. He is dressed (as always for his television broadcasts) in immaculate collar and tie and crisply creased trousers; but he has made his one concession to being a gardener. He has taken off his jacket and is wearing that famous waistcoat with braces just peeping through about the shoulders. Also – as always – he is wearing that wonderful Fred Streeter smile.

Now there is no denying that once you have appeared on television there is an unworthy temptation to feel you have suddenly become someone special. I remember on one occasion interviewing the second Radio Doctor who went by the pseudonym John Anthony Parr; and when the programme was over we travelled together in a crowded train from Shepherds Bush back into Central London.

Looking around the compartment this delightful character expressed sentiments which I believe many of us have known but not admitted. He said, "Do you know, I feel a bit different now. My first time on television. I wonder if it shows! I've half a mind to go round this carriage telling everyone that I've just been on the screen. I can't help feeling that they ought to know!"

I mentioned this story once to Fred and asked him how he had reacted to the sudden onset of 'stardom'. He didn't really give me a direct answer but countered by telling me two more stories.

"There was one of those film actresses – Gloria Swanson I believe it was Frank – who said it was easy for us to get an exaggerated idea of our own importance because we've been on the films or television. But once we're inside those cameras, she said, we're just like tinned sardines. Little things of not much importance! I reckon she'd got the right idea. And then don't let's forget poor old Gilbert Harding. What a character *he* was. But once he became a bit famous, that was really the end of him."

Fred went on to recall that bitter-sweet story of Gilbert being stopped in a Brighton street by an elderly lady who poked him in the ribs and said – 'I can never remember which one you are – is it Richard Dimbleby or Gilbert Harding? You're both so plump.'

'Madam', the affronted Gilbert Harding had replied. 'I am both of them.'

The lady chuckled and retorted: 'Oh I know who you are *now*,' she said. 'You're the rude one.'

It would be tempting to say that with Gardening, Radio and Television on his plate, Fred Streeter could cope with no more. Yet there was another side to his busy life that continued to develop and this was Fred the journalist.

For many years he had been contributing to several specialist gardening journals and to a local newspaper in the Watford area – this having stemmed from his early gardening associations with this particular part of the country. But editors have a wily way of sizing up newcomers to television and of assessing their potential for winning new readers; so when the editor of the Evening Standard saw Fred on television he liked what he saw and decided to act.

"He asked me to nip along to his office and have a word with him Frank, and I got the feeling that we took to each other straight away. Funny old lark when you come to think of it. Thousands of people would have given their eye teeth for the chance to write in one of the big London papers. Yet there was this editor chap saying that some of the other papers were probably after me too – so would I sign up right away and do a regular gardening series for him?"

Fred signed – and soon he had accommodated this new assignment into his weekly routine. Back home at Petworth he would set aside an hour or two each week to write his down-to-earth articles for the *Evening Standard*. This task complete, there was the little matter of planning the content of next week's radio and television shows – before he started to leaf through some of the thousand or more letters he received every month.

His newspaper articles had increased the flow of correspondence and there was no denying that some of the letters and packages he received were not especially welcome.

"One day," Fred recalled, "the postman came stumping up the drive and shouted through the doorway – 'I'm not bringing this lot in here. You'd better come out and fetch it!' So away I went to the doorstep – and you'd never believe the shocking smell that met me. Anyhow I somehow managed to open the little parcel . . . and it was from one of the readers who'd sent me a special type of fungus to identify. Talk about high – it was too far gone for me to start meddling around with it; and I reckon it nearly saw me off as well."

Happier by far was Fred's story of the plovers' eggs. "There was this dear old lady down in the West Country," he explained, "who somehow got it into her head that I doted on plovers' eggs. And regular as clockwork, every season, she'd send me a little gift of plovers' eggs with her very best wishes. Course, I used to reply saying how much I appreciated her kind thought and how much I enjoyed them – though as a matter of fact I can't stand the things. Never could! Then one year the little gift didn't turn up . . . and that was the end of that. We could only suppose the little old lady had died. But – a funny thing you know; although I never touched the eggs, I missed them like anything once they stopped coming."

Nothing, it seemed, could now stop the insistent demands upon Fred's services as writer and broadcaster – though still his first and most demanding job in life was to keep the gardens of Petworth in their customary splendour.

In 1947 Lord Leconfield had conveyed Petworth with a large endowment to the National Trust, while in the private gardens the emphasis moved slowly away from the floral aspects of gardening to give more attention to fruit and vegetables. The area for which Fred had direct responsibility was therefore much reduced; so, too, was the team of workers on whom he could call. Yet still he continued to favour what he always called 'the good old varieties of vegetables'. This could sometimes cause problems in his broadcasts when he would urge his audience to seek out a time-honoured variety that had completely disappeared from the catalogues. Seedsmen would scratch their heads unbelievingly. Then they would say – "I'll bet old Fred Streeter put you on to *that* one!"

Fred was the first to admit that most professional gardeners tend to be inflexible in their views – and first to acknowledge that he himself suffered from this shortcoming! When it was once suggested in a broadcast that the lettuce 'Webb's Wonderful' was the finest in its class, Fred would have none of it. He was strictly a 'Tom Thumb' man. But he was also a great man for championing lost causes; and when he realised that the strange cabbage-like vegetable with a turnip flavour – kohl rabi – was little grown these days, he made it a feature of his very next broadcast.

Charles Wyndham, the Third Baron Leconfield, died in 1952 at the age of eighty. He was just five years older than Fred.

"He'd been a marvellous boss to me Frank and the fairest man you could ever wish to deal with; when I heard he'd gone my first feeling was that it was time to have a quieter life myself. But I still had my health and strength you know and I still had plenty of people who – in a way – seemed to depend on me. So on I went."

Critics can sometimes be harsh on the man who succeeds so well at his chosen career that, almost unbidden, all manner of doors are opened to him. If Capability Brown had been breathing down Fred's neck during the decade that followed the Second World War he might well have said – 'What's all this Fred? Radio ... television ... journalism? I thought you were meant to be a gardener!'

In 1950 Fred answered that unspoken criticism in a most conclusive way. Despite several years away from the cut and thrust of the big Horticultural Shows, he decided it was time to prove to himself (and to anyone else who might be interested), that he had not lost his inimitable touch with flowers.

Deliberately he chose to exhibit at one of the R.H.S.

117

Shows most likely to win the attention of the experts; and in this Show he entered a dazzling display of cyclamen. It proved to be one of the finest displays he had ever created; if confirmation were needed that the old master still kept his skills, this was it.

The display won Fred a Gold Medal and the firm assurance that he was still a wonderful gardener.

Five years later came another honour which gave Fred particular pleasure. For more than forty years he had enjoyed a close friendship with that doyen of rose experts, Harry Wheatcroft. Harry had paid many visits to Petworth; Fred had spent many happy times at the Wheatcroft family home in Nottingham. True, Harry was twenty years younger than Fred but they enjoyed each other's company and – as Harry Wheatcroft recently recalled to me – Fred was always a great raconteur in his quiet way.

"He never tried to impress you with his knowledge," said Harry, "yet if you wanted some really sound advice or an honest opinion on something you'd produced – you could look to Fred, safe in the knowledge that he'd give it to you straight."

Happily, back in 1955, there was a very practical way in which Harry Wheatcroft could express his admiration for Fred. He would name a rose after him. The rose he chose was clear yellow with a delightful and distinctive fragrance. It was developed by crossing the *Luis Brinas* with *Golden Sceptre* and in 'Modern Roses', that encyclopaedia of the rose world, it is classed as having a four-inch flower, a dark foliage and a vigorous growth.

Fashions in roses change as swiftly as clothes' fashions and, although the Fred Streeter Rose enjoyed a spell of popularity, it is none too easy to find these days. This is sad, for it is (as Fred often told me) a rose of good habit and one which blends splendidly with the ever-popular 'Peace'. Harry Wheatcroft is optimistic however that it may be possible to bring back the Fred Streeter Rose . . . which indeed would be a fitting tribute to an old friend.

Fred in his eighties was to continue his radio broadcasts for many years yet; but his career as a regular television performer ended on a rather improbable note. A severe bout of shingles in the late 1950's was the cause.

"I've never felt so ill in all my life," Fred admitted, "and me an old fellow who was known for being pretty tough. I had to call off my broadcasts of course – and the old doctor didn't half read me a curtain lecture. 'You've had just about enough of all these jaunts up to London' he said. 'It's high time you took things a bit quieter. You're not exactly a schoolboy any more; lots of people of your age have been retired for years. So why not give up the television from now on and just stick to the sound radio?'"

Fred took the doctor's advice – though he did accept an invitation to visit Birmingham for the opening of the new television centre there . . . and he did of course resolve to continue with his weekly radio broadcasts.

I am delighted he did. Otherwise I would never have met him!

VIII

"Don't worry Frank — it'll be all right I promise you. I know all the plants and flowers so I'll keep talking about them. You just chip in with a question or two whenever you feel like it!"

Fred spoke those reassuring words to me on the afternoon of our first meeting. We were into the 1960's now and although plans were in hand for the launching of Local Radio, the B.B.C.'s Regional Services — inaugurated before the War and still retaining much of their early character — had several years yet to run. Such a Regional Programme was 'South East' which went on the air after the six o'clock news and had a large and loyal following in the counties bordering London.

It was for 'South East' that I was to make my first broadcast with Fred Streeter and the plan of campaign was simple enough. The programme editor, Marshall Stewart, had suggested that my wife Estelle and I should drive the twenty-two miles or so from our home in Worthing to join Fred and his companion Florrie Hallett at Petworth. The previous year Hilda Streeter had died after a long and distressing illness. Florrie Hallett, Petworth born and bred, and herself a mother and grandmother, had moved skilfully into the role of keeping house for Fred and somehow convincing him that life was still worth living.

Once we had met at Petworth we were all to journey to Guildford – for it was from Guildford Cathedral that we were to make this particular broadcast. The occasion there was a Festival of Flowers and it was proposed that Fred and I should move with our microphone through the Cathedral, conveying to listeners something of the floral splendour spread out before us. This had all the makings of a colourful broadcast, with Fred Streeter the perfect guide.

Before meeting him, I had mentally placed Fred in the setting of some floral Paradise in which he would magically materialise beside a bed of country cottage flowers like lupins and holly-hocks and Canterbury bells. There he would stand a moment, firm but frail, before padding across an emerald lawn to greet us. The reality was very different. The approach we had taken (and were always to take) brought us to the rear of the house. Here we found a wooden outer doorway with a push-button bell to one side. We rang the bell and there was Florrie Hallett – today a firm friend of ours but at the time of our first meeting simply my idea of the perfect person to take good care of a frail and rather vulnerable old gentleman. Tall, greying and with a voice that told of her Sussex origins Florrie was a calm and capable person. She ushered us in to meet the great man – and there he sat in his friendly little kitchen, serene and smiling in a high-back kitchen chair. He was more delicate, more diffident that we had expected. But his voice, for all that we had heard it so many times on the air, was rich and strong.

"Coor, I am pleased to meet you," he said rising to greet

121

Estelle. They shook hands (more formally than they ever did again) then Fred turned to me and enquired – "It's Frank isn't it? I've been hearing all about you."

Beside him on the kitchen table stood a vase of newly cut sweet peas – blue and magenta, lavender and pink. Behind him stood the two-hundred-year old grandfather clock that was to become such a valued time-keeping friend in years to come. Even on this summer's day I could hear the coke crackling busily in the kitchen range. Florrie glanced at the clock, observed that time was getting along and that we should soon be making a move; then she gently eased Fred into his coat and armed him out of the kitchen and into the car.

The drive to Guildford was my first opportunity to learn the particular likes and the dislikes of Fred Streeter. He still enjoyed a drive in the country but did not care for speed on the road. He was inclined to feel the cold these days so, although it was a glorious afternoon, perhaps it would be wise if we kept the windows shut and relied on the ventilators for a breath of fresh air. And yes – Fred's hearing was still surprisingly good but unfortunately his sight was getting a shade misty. One eye in particular was giving him trouble and sometimes he couldn't see much at all with that weaker eye.

During the journey I began to form an opinion of Fred as a near-invalid. Conversation was kept to a polite minimum since I supposed we should conserve Fred's strength for the broadcast that lay ahead. Yet what a transformation came over him when we arrived outside Guildford Cathedral – a triumphantly modern building standing high on a hill in strangely urban surroundings.

Parked in the approach to the Cathedral was the B.B.C. caravan from which the broadcast would be carried by landline to London. And no sooner had we been greeted by our Programme Editor, than Fred the professional took over. Could we, he asked, take a look inside the Cathedral

122

before the broadcast? How long would we have on the air? Was this to be a live or pre-recorded broadcast? Were there any particular aspects of the Festival to which we should give special emphasis? All the skills Fred had garnered in thirty years of radio and television now began to show themselves. My doubts that he was strong enough to sustain such a broadcast began to evaporate – to be replaced by a growing apprehension about my own rôle in the programme. I don't believe I have ever been a particularly diffident broadcaster but I had to admit that the world of plants and flowers held many a trap for young players. And this day I was just such a player!

Fred and I made our preliminary tour of the Cathedral and as the time approached for us to go on the air, more and more worries began to invade my mind. During that tour I had sampled at first hand Fred's encyclopaedic knowledge of every flower in the book and this had served to emphasise how narrow were my own horticultural horizons. How could I be forgiven if I were to give the wrong identity to a plant or flower? Still worse, suppose I could not recognise a particular species at all?

Fred sensed my fears and chuckled at the thought that I could be worried by such a straightforward assignment as this. As he said with good reason, every bud, every blossom, every leaf in that Cathedral was a familiar friend to him; he could chat about any one of them until the end of time; and here was I concerned that we might run out of words in the space of a few brief minutes.

"I'll keep talking Frank," he said, "and you just chip in with a question or two whenever you feel like it! Don't you worry . . . it will be all right! I promise you."

Certainly it was a strange reversal of the customary role of interviewer and interviewee. But Fred managed it brilliantly. There were no awkward pauses . . . no uneasy moments. When we happened upon some plant or bloom that could conceivably baffle me, Fred did not wait for me to grope uneasily for the name. On the contrary he credited me with knowledge far beyond my means and guided our tour with such remarks as – 'Aaah . . . I can see what *you've* spotted over there Frank. Our old friend *Lilium candidum* . . . and what a beauty she is, specially in a marvellous setting like this. And here's something else you'll want me to be talking about. You probably call it the *Hemerocallis* eh? But shall we just give it its nice homely name, the Day Lily? Poor little flower; only lasts a day or two of course and shuts up tight during the night. But cooor . . . what a treat she is while she lasts!'

With a delicate touch and a fine appreciation of the right word at the right time, Fred showed me in those few minutes on the air what sensitive broadcasting is all about. His approach to the microphone was the approach you might make to the attentive ear of a friendly confidant. Our broadcast from Guildford Cathedral was well received. As one Programme Presenter remarked in future years, that first broadcast had some particular warmth which was to make the Frank-and-Fred partnership one of the longest running 'regulars' on sound radio, apart of course from the indomitable Archers and those ever-spinning Desert Island Discs.

Soon after the broadcast I was asked by a Producer in Broadcasting House – "How did you manage to hit it off so well with old Fred, right from the start? You sounded like old friends. We all sensed it you know. But was there some special secret?"

At the time I had no convincing explanation to offer. But looking back to that first meeting and to the long association I was to enjoy with Fred, I believe the key to it all was that I never treated him as an old man. Fred was already in his eighties it's true and it would have been easy to regard him with awe. My approach to him (both on and off the air) was that he was essentially a contemporary, an expert in his own field with a wealth of up-to-the-minute

124

knowledge for today's gardeners. Ask yourself (assuming you haven't yet reached a great old age) how you would feel in your eighties or nineties if you were always approached as a relic of the past . . . something of a phenomenon still to be alive. Consider your reaction to being questioned in over-loud tones, in case your hearing is failing; and in near-basic English for fear that senility is close at hand.

That day of our meeting at Guildford I soon recognised that Fred was failing in none of his faculties. In spite of the warnings about his sight, he identified every plant, every flower in the Cathedral with such instant certainty that any lingering fears were soon set at rest. So when it was suggested a few days later that I should take over the weekly gardening spot with Fred for the 'South East' programme, I decided that there were two important lines of communication now to be firmly established.

Firstly, I must get to know Florrie better. Only by her wonderful efforts had Fred remained so fit and lively. She could guide me in such matters as Fred's particular interests in life – his likes and dislikes. Secondly, I must learn a little more about Fred from those who had already broadcast with him; and who better to consult on that score than John Behague of the B.B.C. who had travelled to Petworth many times to record Fred's gardening hints and tips.

Florrie Hallett is blessed with a good memory and a happy turn of phrase. As a child she had lived 'just over the wall' from the Big House and from the age of six had many glimpses of the legendary Fred Streeter at work. More than this, she had learned of his reputation for being scrupulously fair but undeniably strict.

"The men who worked for him always knew that they couldn't take liberties with Fred Streeter," Florrie recalled. "If he had to go up to London for one reason or another – most likely to make a broadcast – he'd set the men a task before he went and he knew when he returned it would be done just as well as if he'd been watching over them all day.

125

Not many Head Gardeners could say that you know Frank — but Fred could!"

Florrie first got to know Fred Streeter in 1947 when she went to work in the gardens of Petworth House. Knowing his reputation as a disciplinarian, she felt she must apply herself to the work with vigour and determination; and when, that summer's morning, she was set the task of picking blackcurrants, she picked them for all she was worth!

"I was doing fine," Florrie assured me, "Until suddenly we had one of those heavy summer showers. The Heavens seemed to open and I got absolutely soaked. Well of course Mr. Streeter saw all this, so he told me to go into the greenhouse nearby where it was nice and dry and to start pulling up the bamboo canes from the old pea crop."

Florrie was anxious to please — too anxious as it happened. She pulled the first cane out with such energy that it shot straight out of the ground and clean through the roof above her, showering her with broken glass.

"For a moment," said Florrie, "I just wanted to dash back home and burst into tears. I'd been trying so hard, yet I'd done this awful thing on my very first day. But Fred was too quick for me. He'd heard the glass go and he came straight over to discover what had happened. I stood there quaking, feeling like a naughty schoolgirl, yet instead of ticking me off, do you know what he did? He gave me a peach to forget my troubles. And he said 'Don't tell the others will you or they'll all be wanting one!' "

Twenty years later Florrie was to nurse Fred's wife through that last and painful illness when not only did she undergo a major operation on her hip but also lost an eye. Hilda's death in February 1966 came soon after her Diamond Wedding Anniversary. And now with Fred a very old and very lonely man, Florrie began to feel not only affection but a warm and protective love for him. Sometimes, perhaps, she was a little over-protective.

126

"In fact," Florrie once confessed to me, "the day that you and Estelle arrived here to do that first broadcast at Guildford, I wasn't too sure that you were going to hit it off with him. There seemed to be rather a lot of laughter and leg-pulling going on to my way of thinking. But I soon realised that Fred had really taken to the two of you and he began to look forward to you coming. It seemed to give him a new interest in life."

Meanwhile, from John Behague of the B.B.C. I learned of another side to Fred's character – that he simply hated to disappoint anyone. Even until quite late in life he would insist on giving a personal greeting to the many listeners and viewers who chose to visit him unbidden at Petworth. It was not unknown for a knock to come on the cottage door on a mid-winter's night and for a hopeful visitor to announce that he happened to be passing that way and could Fred Streeter spare him just a few minutes.

Almost without exception the answer was 'yes'! And almost without exception those few minutes extended into an hour or more! One of John's most treasured stories of Fred concerned an elderly blind lady who paid him a visit on a blissfully peaceful evening in high summer.

"Fred greeted her at the door," said John, "took her into the cottage for a chat, and then asked if she would care for a short stroll in the gardens. Of course, she wouldn't be able to see the plants and flowers herself, but she could enjoy the wonderful evening scents of the garden . . . and Fred would be proud to be her guide. Naturally the old lady was overjoyed and together they spent half an hour or so enjoying the delights of the garden to the full. But as their trip came to an end she said to Fred – 'It's all been so marvellous Mr. Streeter . . . there's only one other thing that could make this my perfect evening. Some time ago in a broadcast you mentioned a dear old robin that would pay you a visit here and would sit on the freshly turned soil while you sowed your seeds. Wouldn't it be wonderful if that robin could visit us tonight and give us a song?' "

"Now Fred was never a pessimist. But he knew full well
that his robin had long ago left this world for Bird Paradise
or wherever it is that all good robins go. But somehow the
Bird Community got the message that evening and out
from the bushes came the most marvellous birdsong imaginable . . . the voice of a robin with a spectacular sense of
occasion.

As Fred stood and marvelled at how this could be, the
blind lady turned to him and said – 'You see Mr. Streeter,
miracles *do* sometimes happen, especially in your garden!' "

Such stories were good background knowledge for me
before our next broadcast together. To add a suitably rural
note, it was suggested that we should make our recordings
in the garden whenever possible. The background song of a
blackbird or even the distant sound of a garden fork at
work would lend depth and colour to whatever we had to
say.

So it was that our little party – Fred and Florrie, Estelle
and I – gathered at the cottage early one Thursday morning then made our way down the gravel driveway, past the
vegetable garden and along to the sunken garden. Here we
were sheltered from the breezes that still persist on even the
sultriest of summer days, and can play havoc with a microphone. Yet we were within earshot of any sounds of the
garden that might come our way.

Close by the sunken garden stood a little summer house
full of summery things like balding tennis balls, tennis rac-
quets with sagging strings, metal trays still bearing the
sticky rings of the fruit drink glasses that had been served
on them, and folding canvas seats which take exasperating
minutes to set up yet collapse in a single second.

Fred pointed to the summer house and said – "P'raps
you can nip in there Frank and fetch a few seats; then we
can set up nice and cosy down here and really enjoy ourselves."

128

Estelle eased Fred into the only seat with arm-rests while Florrie distributed the drinks she had brought from the cottage: for Fred his accustomed glass of blackcurrant juice; for Estelle a glass of grapefruit juice; for me, a dry sherry.

With the tape recorder settled on the grass and the microphone angled slightly towards Fred, all was ready for our rural show to begin. And as Fred's voice filled the Sunken Garden that he himself had created, it was strange to think that these same words would be reaching out to gardeners who'd pruned their first roses or planted their first hopeful rows of radishes close on eighty years after Fred tended that first tiny garden of his just down the road at Pulborough.

Many of Fred's most dedicated followers wanted to know more about his broadcasting technique. Did he have a script? Did we rehearse each question and answer with split-second precision? Was Fred knee-deep in reference books, for how else could he remember all those botanical terms? And – being so elderly – did he really have such a powerful, jolly voice or was it some piece of electronic trickery that transformed a whisper into the rollicking voice that came over the air?

The Fred I knew was certainly no man for scripts! He had a script, we know, in that original broadcast with C. H. Middleton. Perhaps he referred to the occasional note in later broadcasts, when it was helpful to have an *aide memoire*. As for reference books, lesser gardeners may lean heavily on the words of others; they may seek written confirmation for every move they make. Not Fred. Some folk in this world are said to know all the answers, but Fred was the only man I've met who really did. From his still sharp mind he would conjure such names as *Anemone alpina sulphurea* or *Passiflora caerulea*. Then he would gently remind us that we may know them better as a specially beautiful anemone and a wondrous Passion Flower! He never made a great show of the knowledge he possessed, but

129

possess it he most certainly did.

And what of that voice? There was no electronic trickery to give it added power. In ordinary conversation, Fred was fairly soft-spoken. But he was also a showman in the best tradition – and the moment the microphone was live he would lend his voice that extra element of projection which makes for a forceful broadcast. He understood the light and shade of voice production. He knew about timing too. And when he said 'Just give your runner beans a little bit of mulch. Cooor . . . they'll thank you from the bottom of their hearts,' there was just that barely perceptible pause between sentences that gave his listeners a chance to get the message. It was tricks like that made folk stop and listen when Fred Streeter was on the air.

Those were the days when his broadcasts were being heard only in the programme *South East*. And though we had planned to continue making our recordings in the sanctuary of the sunken garden, Progress was beginning to catch up with us.

Petworth isn't far from Gatwick Airport, and no sooner would Fred be in full flood about the rich, coppery foliage of *Fuchsia Thalia* or the delicate delights of *Iris stylosa* than a low flying jet would make its breathless passage across the sky, drowning even the sturdy Sussex tones of Fred Streeter.

"Let's go into the kitchen instead Frank," he suggested one morning. "It's quiet and cosy in there. It should make a nice little studio and we won't be interrupted like this."

A thick cloth was placed on the kitchen table to prevent echo from the surface. Then on the cloth we set our microphone stand. The heavy pendulum of the grandfather clock was halted so that its tick should not punctuate our broadcast; and we even turned down the heat control of the kitchen range so that the bubblings of Florrie's lunchtime stew should not disturb the quiet background we were creating.

130

Finally, Fred settled himself in his high-backed chair, Florrie placed a shawl around his shoulders, and the stage was set for another edition of 'The Frank-and-Fred Show'.

"Now this week," Fred said before recording got under way, "I thought we'd talk about the right way to treat the tulips and the daffodils Frank. Some people seem to think that both of them thrive on exactly the same sort of treatment. Not a bit of it . . . and that's the main point I want to make."

With a broad outline like this, Fred introduced me to the basic topic for our discussion. Then he went on to enlarge on the theme and suggest specific questions I might put to him.

"You see Frank, with the daffodils you want to leave the foliage on as long as possible. For instance, if you've planted some drifts of daffodils in your lawn and you want to make it nice and tidy once the daffs have finished flowering, for goodness sake don't run the mower over them a week or two after the flowers have faded. If you do . . . you'll spoil next season's growth. But with the tulips, it's a different matter. You want to have their heads off just as soon as the flowers begin to wilt!"

Rarely did we stick to a single topic in a broadcast, on the basis that by casting our net a bit wider we would be interesting a greater number of listeners. So on this occasion Fred suggested that we should also answer the listener who was anxious to grow leeks "just like those miners up in Northumberland do." "That'll give me a chance," said Fred with satisfaction, "to tell him that leeks love plenty of manure and plenty of bonemeal – and to sow them at stations, three seeds to a station, thinning down to just one seedling as they develop. And whatever he does, he must make sure that the soil is nice and fine. Then as his plants develop, he should hoe the soil regularly and make sure it never gets dry. That way he'll get some lovely leeks – enough to make those miners up in the North go green with

131

envy!"

Five minutes of discussion along these lines was all the preparation we ever needed. No script. No detailed notes of any sort. Simply a growing awareness that we knew precisely what was expected of one another and had an instinctive feel for what we believed to be a successful broadcast in the 'Frank-and-Fred' tradition.

It was not difficult to imagine why elderly and middle-aged gardeners would make a point of tuning in each week. Fred was a voice of their times; their earliest memories of gardening had been linked with the name of Streeter. But as our partnership developed, more and more young listeners came into our orbit too and sometimes we would take account of this by angling a broadcast especially to them.

Fred was a great believer in giving children their own plot of land to cultivate. He had no time for the parent so proud of his garden that he couldn't bear to see a child setting foot on the table-top lawn or toddling within sniffing distance of his seedlings.

"Do you know Frank," he would confide in his best admonishing tones, "I've even heard Dads saying 'Don't you get on there son – and don't you go near that!' the very moment a poor little chap has poked his nose outside the back door. That's not the way to go about it at all!"

He held up his hands, as he sometimes would, to capture the horror of the situation.

"No . . . here's what to do! As soon as they start to show an interest, give them their own little plot of ground. Needn't be more than six feet square if they're only youngsters. Then say to them 'That's your very own land. Your first garden. See what you can grow on it'"

"But starting them young like that, what would you advise them to grow?" I asked.

"Well most children like quick results," he replied. "And most of them like something tasty to eat. So why not buy them a packet of radish seed for a start? Then perhaps a few

132

lettuces. And because children love the excitement of things that grow tall, how about a few runner beans? They can always get Dad to lend them some bean poles . . . but here's a word of warning when putting them in. Never cross the bean poles at the top like some people do. That's all wrong. Let each pole go straight up on its own. If you start crossing them at the top, the poor old beans get in a terrible muddle and don't know which way to go!"

No sooner had Fred given this advice on the air than many children – and parents too – wrote in to suggest that we should devote more time to young listeners. There were even some disenchanted Dads who later wrote to say that their little boy or girl had duly been given a plot to cultivate; and while they loved the seed sowing bit and couldn't wait to start harvesting the crops, the down-to-earth matter of digging didn't go down nearly as well. What was to be done?

"Well," said Fred, "there's a simple answer to that one too! I've already told you that children love quick results . . . and enjoy a crop they can get their teeth in. But haven't you noticed that they thrive on a bit of competition too? So why not arrange for the children of the house to have a competition among themselves to see who can keep the best garden . . . with Mum as the judge? Of course, if there's only one kiddie in the house, he can have a competition with Dad!"

"And how about a prize for the winner?"

"Well that's an easy one Frank; a few packets of seeds of course! And perhaps the promise of one of old Fred Streeter's yarns as a bedtime story."

Quite apart from straight gardening advice, Fred loved recounting some of his favourite tales to young people and one of these concerned the landlady of a Sussex pub who was renowned for the succulence of her rabbit pie.

"She was a trusting soul," Fred explained, "and she'd place the pie at one end of the bar counter so that the chaps

133

— mainly gardeners from the estate — could help themselves. The only trouble was that those chaps weren't all that well off, and the poor old landlady soon discovered that far more pie was being taken than was ever paid for!"

"Well after a few weeks of this she couldn't stand it any longer and as luck would have it an old tom cat had died that morning in the pub's back yard. So she fetched the sharpest knife she could find and skinned the creature — then went into the bar, brandishing it for all she was worth. 'There', she said, to the chaps from the bothy. 'You've been wondering all this time how I could afford to serve you lot with rabbit pie, yet get hardly a penny piece for my pains. Rabbit pie be blowed! It's a very different sort of meat you've been eating . . . and you'd better have the rest of it now'. And she threw the old tom cat's skin towards them."

There is a rather poignant post-script to this tale. For when John Behague retold it to a group of ladies at the Ferring Women's Institute, he reached his triumphant punchline then stood back awaiting gales of laughter. Unfortunately he was speaking to a group of inveterate cat lovers.

Another of Fred's much-loved yarns involved a couple of elderly ladies who asked very humbly if they might take a look round the fruit gardens of Petworth. So diffident were they that Fred not only agreed to their request but decided to give them a few of the fallen apples to take home.

"As these dear old souls started to load their baskets," he recalled, "one of them turned to me and said — "By-the-by, I'm told that Fred Streeter, the Radio Gardener lives here. I suppose there's no chance of getting a peep at him is there?' 'Oooh!' I said, 'Not a hope I'm afraid. And anyhow, he wouldn't half create if he saw you with all those apples. He's a bit of a miserable old so-and-so I'm afraid.' Well that was enough for them Frank. Off they scampered with their scrumps, never dreaming that all the time they'd been face to face with that miserable old so-and-so!"

Yet it wasn't only in the realms of children and elderly ladies that Fred found his most devoted audiences. One of Britain's best-loved writers (and a skilful gardener in his own right) was also an unfailing weekly listener to Fred. He was H. E. Bates, and in 1971, when Volume II of his Autobiography 'The Blossoming World' was published, I was asked to visit his home in Kent to record a radio interview with him.

He and his wife Madge lived in the village of Little Chart and here – with a deal of skill and several touches of sheer inspiration – they had converted an old granary into a home which escaped triumphantly from the strait-jacket of conventionality. And in the garden where Estelle and I sat with this delightful couple, enjoying tea and scones and strawberry jam, Bates had created his own particular wonderland. With much hard labour (and not a little help from his friends) he had made the rockery of which he had always dreamed. It was a living, exciting thing with its moss-covered Kentish rag-stone – not, as he once wrote, like many a rock-garden 'which resembles the grave of some dead elephant stuck about with naked tombstones.'

Yet in his Autobiography, Bates tells with all his sensitive awareness of nature, how he and Madge first looked upon the ruined farmyard that was to become their garden. Their first glimpse had evinced dismay that came near to despair. 'In it stood a decaying haystack. Beside it stood a decaying willow – and beside that another. Piles of rock and rubble lay strewn about in this forest of dock, grass and thistles.'

It was from all this that he was to create a joyous garden of brightness and colour and from which he was to give Estelle a little shrub with glossy leaves and tiny, unpretentious pink flowers, the name of which we have never known but which we always call 'Our H. E. Bates plant.' And it was typical of this talented and friendly man that he should say to me – 'Of course Frank you're the chap who talks to dear old Fred Streeter each week. Well there's something I want you to tell old Fred. I'm no genius when it comes to gardening . . . but his advice is the straightforward sort of stuff I can follow. And it's thanks to him that I have a garden I can really enjoy all the year round. See . . . the perennial asters are still blooming. So are the dahlias and salvias. In fact, if Fred ever decides to give up broadcasting (and I hope he never does) I'd love to follow in his footsteps! I think I'd make a good radio gardener because I'm a simple soul at heart.' With that, Bates picked up a copy of his book *A Love of Flowers* and wrote these words on the fly leaf: 'Best wishes from Bert – successor to Fred.'

I told Fred of the admiration that this garden-loving author had for him and it was even tentatively suggested that one day the two of them – Fred and 'Bert' – might meet for a broadcast together. As the man in the middle with the microphone, what an opportunity I would have had to match the sensitive romanticism of H. E. Bates with the solid earthiness of Fred.

Sadly, Bates died early in 1975 so these particular dreams never came true. But – on a happier note – it was early in the 1970's that Frank and Fred won promotion!

The early morning weekday programme 'Today' had been extended to Saturday mornings too; and since, under the proposals of the far-reaching document *Broadcasting in the 70's* the *South East* programme had come to a close, our weekly gardening chats were now given a regular Saturday morning slot in *Today* and our audience was nation-wide.

These were the days when the programme was still being presented by Jack de Manio and on 25th June we celebrated Fred's birthday on the air. Florrie had ordered a primrose-decorated birthday cake from the local Petworth baker while a second cake was made by John Behague's wife – for she and her husband still visited Fred regularly and made a particular point of never missing his

136

birthday.

By this stage of his life Fred had made one small concession in his rigorous abstention from alcohol. The doctor had suggested that a drop of whisky in his tea might give him a timely lift, especially those mornings when he was due to broadcast; no hefty slug of liquor, just a teaspoonful or two by way of reinforcement. Fred tried it and liked what he tried. So Estelle and I decided that a suitable birthday gift would be a bottle of Scotch.

This was the first occasion we had ever visited Fred on his birthday, and what we discovered when we arrived at Petworth was a surprise we shall never forget. The white-painted dining room was always light and bright and welcoming. Even in high summer there was usually a fire in the grate and its light would be reflected from the ranks of polished brassware on the mantelpiece and the window sills and even on the very walls themselves. But today this was an extra-special birthday room. On the table and sideboard and every conceivable ledge were the birthday cards that had come flooding in from listeners all over Britain – some even from France and Holland and Belgium. Several of the cards and many of the Greetings Telegrams had been addressed simply to Fred Streeter, Petworth. Others carried the still more basic address – Fred Streeter, England. As the postman put it to me at the time 'If there *is* another Fred Streeter in England, we've never heard of him.'

Many of the cards were unblushingly romantic in their messages. Love came in rich measure from almost every envelope that was opened. Some of the senders insisted that Fred was such a solidly British institution that he must never dream of retiring from the radio but must go on broadcasting long past his century. There was even one card from a lady in the West Country who believed that Fred had saved her life. If it had not been for his comforting words about the companionship that comes from a bowl of sweet-scented bulbs in a once lonely room, she was

137

convinced that she would have put an end to herself.

Some of our particularly successful broadcasts were transcribed for rebroadcasting overseas; and although it must have seemed strange for the listener in Malta or Cyprus or Singapore to hear homespun advice about the care of an English country garden – the mere fact that Fred was deeply immersed in his Petworth cauliflowers and cabbages and carrots brought to many who tuned in a wonderful breath of home.

Fred received birthday greetings from a British nurse serving in Singapore; and by a quirk of fate this same nurse was later to return not only to England but to Petworth Cottage Hospital – where she took care of Fred during one of his brief stays there.

Marshall Stewart – who was now the Editor of the 'Today' programme – came down from Broadcasting House for Fred's birthday, bringing with him another bottle of Scotch and for Florrie a huge box of chocolates. Lord Egremont who had succeeded his uncle Lord Leconfield as owner of Petworth would be calling later in the day to pay his respects. And then there was the cutting of the cake and the opening of the champagne – this part of the ceremony being recorded so that it could be broadcast in the 'Today' programme the following morning.

And so it was. In fact, the opening of that champagne produced such a cracking report that Jack de Manio was heard to comment – 'Just for a moment I thought Frank had shot him!'

It was around this time that a new catch-phrase came into common currency. We had been using it for months without realising that it had such a special appeal. It had started in a humble way but soon it was recognised everywhere; so much so that when one morning this particular phrase was cut from the 'Frank-and-Fred' broadcast because we had over-run our time, complaining phone calls poured into Broadcasting House and we knew that we had found precisely the right words for our weekly 'sign-off'.

It went something like this . . . "Well Fred," I would say, "what with planting out the tomatoes, sowing another row of lettuces and rooting the strawberry runners, you've given us plenty to keep us out of mischief this week. Just time for me to say Cheers for Now!" Then Fred would allow a split-second pause before replying "Ho! Ho! Ho! Ho! Cheerio Frank . . . Cheerio Everybody!"

Listeners would write to say that Saturday morning wasn't complete without that rollicking 'Cheerio' from Fred. Some would insist that it burst upon their loud-speakers with such force that they always had to rush over to their radios and turn down the volume. Children in the street would take a knowing, sidelong glance at me and then roar 'Cheerio Frank . . . Cheerio Everybody.' And on leaving my local in the evenings, no longer was I given a tol-erably formal goodnight! It was 'Cheerio Frank' in the true Fred Streeter tradition.

Many people have put it to me that this must have been a carefully contrived 'sign-off' – the result of all sorts of vocal trial and error. It was nothing of the kind. It just happened.

Fred, as ever, had found the right words for the occasion. And the right way of saying them.

IX

"Some folk are almost hypnotised by the spade and fork Frank. They reach for them every time they set foot in the garden. Cooor . . . they can easily do more harm than good. But when it comes to the dear old hoe — now that's another kettle of fish altogether!"

Fred was no man for riding hobby horses. But he wasn't beyond taking the occasional dig at the advocates of deep digging; for it was his firm belief that a great deal of time is wasted in over-zealous digging, especially in well established gardens that have long since been cleared of all the builder's rubble to which so many new plots are heir. On the other hand, where digging is really imperative, his advice was to get it started good and early. Procrastination is as big a thief of time in the garden as anywhere else on earth.

"Take the chap who's just moved into a new garden or allotment towards the end of summer," he'd explain, "he'll be tempted to say to himself 'No need to do much digging till spring. Plenty of time for *that* when the winter's over.' What a dreadful mistake that is! Take my tip and get the soil nice and open before the weather gets really cold; then the frosts will do half the work for you because frost is a wonderful soil conditioner. And here's another reason for getting the rough digging done in the autumn. Suppose we get one of those springs when it keeps on raining for weeks on end. You won't be able to set foot on the garden . . . you'll get weeks behind all your neighbours and that will never do!"

Fred was a great conservationist long before the word became such common currency; and just as he would counsel us to make profitable use of every square inch of garden, so he would find a good use for many of Nature's cast-offs.

"Let's look at that little business of sweeping up the leaves in the autumn Frank. First thing to do, once you've got your broom or your besom out of the shed, is to see which way the wind is blowing. Yes . . . I really mean it. Then be sure to sweep *with* the wind. You'd be surprised how many gardeners forget that simple tip and as soon as they get to the end of the garden and think the job's nearly done, all the leaves have blown back to where the poor chap started."

In the matter of converting leaves into leaf mould, Fred had one word of warning. Never include horse chestnut leaves in your heap because they contain a particularly unpleasant acid which the soil won't welcome. But remembering that one exception, pile your leaves into an evergrowing heap, sprinkling a little sulphate of ammonia between each layer. This speeds up the process of decomposition and promises you a really first-rate supply of leaf mould the following year. And as Fred once put it, leaf mould is jolly good-natured stuff; it makes heavy soil lighter and helps light soil retain its moisture. So the time you spend in leaf sweeping certainly pays good dividends.

141

"Once you've got that little job under way," Fred would warn, "don't imagine that you can take things easy just because it's autumn. Not a bit of it. As soon as the frost has paid a visit to the dahlias, lift them carefully out of the ground, comb out any loose soil from between the tubers; turn them upside down to let any moisture drain away; then store them in a nice safe place, well away from the damp and the frost. And while you've still got your gumboots on, you'd better start sowing a few vegetables for next spring Frank."

Advice like this often came as a surprise to listeners who were new to Fred's approach to gardening. They looked upon autumn as the time to put up the gardening shutters and to dismiss all idea of sowings. But early in November Fred would urge them to make a sowing of Aqua Dulce Broad Beans and a few of the famous Feltham First Peas as well. With a little foresight like this the first beans and peas should be ready for cropping the following May. In other words, right through those seemingly barren months of winter, germination is quietly progressing below the surface where the frost's probing fingers cannot penetrate.

Strange to say, some of the trips to Petworth I recall with especial affection were visits made in the brief, grey days of Winter when Fred would recapture the mounting excitement that every true gardener feels as Christmas draws near.

"What a time we had in the old days Frank when we knew that the big house would be bristling with people at Christmas time. Once we'd safely pruned the fruit trees and given them a nice tar-oil spray in early December, it was time to start making up the Christmas wreaths and to plan all the other decorations we'd be having. Now I expect you're going to ask me which is my favourite Christmas flower; it must be the lovely Christmas Rose. So here's what to do if you want to have some of these glistening little roses on *your* dinner table this Christmas. Grow a few

142

plants close under a wall and as soon as the buds start showing in November, put four little sticks around each plant.
Then place a sheet of glass over them, supported by the
sticks. That'll protect the flowers as they develop you see,
even if we get heavy winds or rains, and you'll have a wonderful display of roses to welcome old Santa Claus on
Christmas Day!"

Looking back down the years, Fred could recall a long
succession of Christmas Days when he'd scarcely had time
to think of his own festivities, so hot was the pace in the
garden. When I asked him once on the air how he would
like to see the Nation's gardeners spending their Christmas
Day he soon made it clear that this was to be no day of rest
for them.

"First off," he said, "you gardeners can settle in front of
the fire after breakfast and get out your seed catalogue for
an hour or so. There's no time like Christmas Day for
drawing up your seed order. After all, once Christmas is
over you'll have so much to keep you occupied that you
won't have any time for paper work."

Fred went on to remind us that once the seeds arrive we
must firmly resist the temptation to peep inside the packets
but should keep them tight sealed until they're needed.
Otherwise by opening those packets we're extending a
warm invitation to the mice and the beetles to take a nibble
at all the seeds they fancy. What's more, we must always
store our seeds in a dry, cool spot – "Not in some leaky old
shed," Fred chuckled, "where the rain drips in and makes a
lovely seed soup!"

But then it was back to the chores for Christmas Day
itself; and though he had started the day for us on a reasonably quiet note, he was soon to have us out in the open.

"Now most of us have had the guilty feeling on
Christmas afternoon that we've been a bit too fond of the
turkey and plum pudding . . . so here's what I want you to
do *this* Christmas. Instead of having that second helping of

143

pudding and that extra mince pie, spend just one hour in the garden. It'll soon slip by, and you can catch up with the festivities later on in the day. But out in the garden you can get busy putting a few old boxes or buckets over the rhubarb crowns to force them along a bit; and you can dig over that neglected little patch of soil that's been looking so sorry for itself. Then as soon as the daylight fades – indoors you can go, feeling a thousand times better than if you'd nodded off in the armchair!''

So much for the gardener's Christmas Day! And once Christmas was over and the dank, dark months of January and February were on the calendar, this was not only the time to send the shears and the secateurs and the mowers away for sharpening but it was also parsnip planting time in Fred's book.

"This is where I'm going to get all Tender and True," he would explain; "because that's the best variety of parsnip I know. Now if, like many gardeners, you've never had much luck with parsnips, here's what I suggest. Get a nice big metal rod (a crowbar some folk would call it) and make several holes in the soil about three feet deep. Fill them almost up to the top with lovely fine soil, then plant three parsnip seeds at each of those stations. As soon as you see them sprouting, decide which of the three seedlings looks the best, discard the other two, and let the prize specimen grow on. With all that fine soil beneath him, he'll go burrowing down and down – and I promise you'll have the straightest, cleanest parsnips you've ever grown. By the by, if you're a bit unlucky with your carrots as well, try this same dodge of planting them at stations too . . . only you ought to wait until the end of March before you start sowing your carrots.''

Fred was never a pessimistic gardener and in the early months of each new year he would confidently predict that a record-breaking growing season lay in store for us.

"If you're lucky enough to have a greenhouse," he'd say,

144

"then February is the time to start sowing your antirrhinums and your petunias. And if you want to keep on the right side of the wife, I'd sow some indoor lettuces as well. The best ones I know for indoor sowing just now are Fortune and Unrivalled, but have a word with your seedsman and he'll tell you which varieties do best in your neighbourhood."

"And what about one or two outdoor jobs in February," I asked, knowing well that he would always have something pretty taxing to keep the gardener out of mischief.

"Well this is the very time of year to take a look at the rockery Frank. More than likely the rain has washed some of the soil away from the surface-rooting plants like the daisies and aubretia. So first of all make good those losses with a bit of compost and be sure that everything is nice and firm, ready to make a real burst of growth now that spring is on the way!"

Now although Fred's philosophy was always to keep us busy in the garden, he was quick to warn us against getting on the soil in the early months of the year if it was still inclined to be on the sticky side. Only after we'd had a few dry days were the signals at green for our first steps on to the lawn — beginning with a thorough sweeping to remove the winter's debris, followed by a light raking to let in the air.

"When you've done that Frank, don't dare to start mowing will you? That'll have to wait for quite a few weeks yet . . . though soon you can sow some grass seed in any bare patches that you've uncovered on the lawn. Now I know I'm always telling you not to sow seed thickly; but there are two big exceptions to that rule. When you're sowing mustard and cress and when you're sowing grass seed. So don't stint when you fill in those bare patches on the lawn. By being generous with the seed the old sparrows can have a nice feed of it and still leave plenty to start growing!"

145

February is also onion sowing time, and Fred was among the many gardeners who are convinced that an onion a day does more to keep the doctor away than the much vaunted apple.

"When I first went to work as a boy," he recalled, "the old gardeners were so keen on their onions and garlic that they'd eat an onion just like you and I might eat an apple. What's more they'd even tuck a clove of garlic in their sock when they got dressed in the morning and leave it there all day. And here's an amazing thing: when they went to kiss the wife goodnight she'd say 'You've been eating garlic dear haven't you?', even though the poor fellow had done nothing of the sort. What had happened was that the oil from the garlic had penetrated into the skin and got properly into the circulation. It's like that you know . . . really gets into your system."

"But you were going to tell us about *planting* the onions," I reminded Fred.

"So I was," he said, "and the big secret with onions is to prepare a bed for them back in November – nice and deep with plenty of manure, because the old onion is a proper heavy feeder. Now when February is nearly over, make that bed good and firm and sow your seed about a quarter of an inch deep as soon as we get a nice dry day. Of course, if you want to take the easy way out, why not buy some of those onion sets that are so popular these days? You just shove the little bulbs in, about six inches apart, leaving a foot between rows. They'll root away like billyho! But a funny thing is that no matter how carefully you plant them, there'll be one or two little bounders that come popping out of the ground like corks. So keep a watch on the bed for the first few days, just to make sure they've all settled in safely!"

Now I wonder how many of today's gardeners have ever made use of a hotbed? According to Fred, some of the hotbeds he made in his apprentice days were most elaborate affairs, built in shallow pits and containing a rich blend of strawy horse manure to get them started in life; but the type he advised for his small garden listeners was simpler in concept with ingredients well within every gardener's reach. Greenstuff of almost any sort is grist to the hotbed mill! The outside leaves of cabbages and sprouts – unwanted in the kitchen – are just the things on which the hotbed will thrive, mixed in with generous helpings of leaf mould. Farmyard manure is another splendid ingredient, though clearly not easy to come by in the typical suburban situation. The bed can be made either on the surface of the soil or built up from a shallow pit; in any event it shuld be turned at least two or three times during its formative days and allowed to rise to a height of about four feet. Each time the bed is turned, it should be treated to a sprinkling of sulphate of ammonia.

The whole idea of the hotbed (best made during February or early March) is to provide a warm and welcoming site on which early, out-of-season vegetables can be grown. Used correctly, it will advance a crop by at least a month or six weeks – but the one big pitfall to be avoided is the fierce and sometimes damaging heat that rotting greenstuff and manure will generate. So when the bed is nearing completion, be sure to allow any steam to escape and then (if you have a suitable thermometer) carefully check that the bed-temperature is no higher than 75°Farenheit, (23·8 degrees Centigrade).

This is the moment to top off the bed with a layer of finely sifted soil – the depth of that soil being gauged to suit the type of vegetables you plan to plant. Marrows, cucumbers and capsicum were three crops that Fred especially singled out as hotbed candidates, but early carrots, beetroots and cauliflowers are equally suitable.

"Funny," said Fred, "How traditional things like the good old hotbed don't seem so popular these days. And I'll tell you another thing. There's many a new gardener who'll plan a lovely garden today without giving a thought to one of the most important things; the herb garden!"

In Fred's book there should be nothing formal about the herb garden. He conceived it as a colourful and attractive feature of the garden – rather in the manner of a rockery, with half a dozen smallish stones, two at the back and four in front, to provide what he called 'punctuation marks' in the siting of the herbs.

Within this framework the herbs should be planted in groups, taking care to include such stars of the herbal show as thyme and parsley; chives and borage; and of course the vitally necessary mint. Purple sage was another of his favourites for Fred maintained that no sausage was complete without that subtle hint of sage.

During all the hundreds of broadcasts I made with him, only once can I recall him being guilty of a factual error – and even that was more by way of a slip of the tongue, a momentary lapse of concentration. This was when he described borage (a herb much used for decorating fruit cups) as having a yellow flower. Dozens of admonishing letters arrived within the next few days saying that he had erred a little from the path of righteousness. There was even one letter which stated the case in quite poetic terms:

Rue is yellow,
Tansy is too;
Balm is lemon
But borage is blue!

In the following week's broadcast, Fred did penance for his error by promising never again to allow borage to fly under false colours. But he did not neglect to mention that though borage is usually blue it can occasionally produce a flower of delicate pink.

To Fred's mind May was a month of miracles in the garden, with most of those miracles coming in little packets of seeds! "Yet here's a funny thing Frank," he would add. "Most folk seem to turn into millionaires once they get a packet of seeds in their hands. They sow so lavishly that the poor little things can't germinate and get choked in the rush. So remember never to pour your seeds straight from the packet into the bed; you can't control the flow that way. Better by far to pour a few into the palm of your hand and then to sprinkle them in with your fingers."

That same sin of over-lavishness was also to be found, said Fred, in the way that many gardeners use the watering-can:

"Take the Brussels Sprouts for instance," he explained. "I always like to see them safely planted out in their final quarters by the fourth week in May and it's important to settle them in really firmly. But, once they're in they should be given one good watering and no more. You'll see some gardeners who're always at them with the watering can. They can't seem to leave the poor little things alone. The result is big leaves and bursted Brussels — and that's no good to anyone. So don't be heavy handed with the water . . . but do remember to sprinkle a little lime around the soil now and then, just to keep it good and fresh."

Providing the soil is reasonably rich and the plants have plenty of space, there should be no problems in growing successful Brussels Sprouts. Fred's favourite variety was 'Fillbasket' and his crops usually did just that! Much more temperamental — and highly susceptible to variations in soil conditions and climate — are cauliflowers. And that's why Fred advised us to treat them sweetly.

"Of course," he said, "no one's suggesting that the cauliflower is the easiest vegetable to rear. It likes rich, well manured soil and plenty of water whenever the going gets hot. But I really do believe in treating them sweetly Frank — by sprinkling a teaspoonful of sugar around the roots now and again."

This sugar treatment was Fred's formula for producing

the firm, dazzling white heart or 'curd' in a cauliflower which is every gardener's dream. He used it with especial success on the exhibition cauliflowers he grew for some of the most exalted shows in the country; and although this sort of treatment may seem an unforgivable extravagance today, many gardeners who heard this advice on the air carried out the interesting experiment of feeding sugar to one or two of their cauliflower plants, while leaving the rest of the crop as 'controls'. The verdict was that a teaspoonful of sugar not only helps the medicine go down, but persuades cauliflowers to grow in the most delightful way!

"So there," said Fred, with evident satisfaction. "I've shown you that cauliflowers have a sweet tooth. But did you know that runner beans love a diet of newspapers?"

Fred knew full well that remarks like these were sure-fire conversation stoppers; he loved to hear how listeners would be halted in the middle of their cornflake breakfasts or transfixed in the course of shaving the moment he produced his latest improbable comment on the air!

"Don't get me wrong," he would continue, "it's not that those runner beans can *read*. It's simply that they make the perfect lining for your bean trench before you top it up with compost and soil. The newspapers hold moisture splendidly, so even if we get a long, dry spell, the moisture from the rotting paper will steadily seep into the growing roots and help to keep them fit and healthy."

Having heard this explanation, no doubt I looked suitably impressed because old Fred gave me a knowing wink and added — "Of course, if you like your beans with plenty of sauce, you'd better give them those cheeky newspapers with one or two pin-ups. That should keep them happy down there in the trench!"

With the coming of June and the long summer evenings, Fred liked to imagine that many of the 'City gents' among his listeners would be dashing home from the office, snatching a perfunctory bite to eat, clambering into the oldest of clothes and then making straight for the garden.

"So much to be done," Fred urged, "that the poor chap has no time for a proper meal. Never mind. If he's had a bit too much to eat and drink with his business friends at lunchtime, we'll soon get his waistline slimmed down again."

Those long summer evenings Fred saw as the golden opportunity for major garden projects such as building a new path. His favourite path was the gravel variety rolled down so firmly (especially after a shower of rain) that the surface becomes as smooth and hard as concrete. As for concrete paths themselves, he had no time for them.

"Too cold and too uninteresting," he maintained. "And if you get a spell of rain, it flushes straight over the surface and makes it like glass. Can be a real death trap Frank, especially for the elderly."

Crazy paving he saw as another potential hazard, though he was quick to admit that a well planned 'crazy' pathway can add an interesting new dimension to many a garden. For safety's sake it is vitally important to keep these pathways utterly level and this is best done by running a board over the surface as each stone is placed in position. Moreover, to see crazy paving to best advantage, the gaps should be filled with suitably hardy little plants – even herbs – to add colour and interest.

Yet, while Fred was busy telling us what to plant in our pathways, there were whole armies of listeners who were battling to do quite the reverse; they were trying to get rid of unwanted weeds, especially on open-surface paths. Some had tried proprietary weedkillers as the rational answer to the problem, but had found them expensive and of only short-term benefit. Others had used sodium chlorate but had been forced to admit that this vicious chemical isn't merely a killer of weeds but of more or less everything that comes in its way.

"No doubt about it," said Fred, "sodium chlorate is

wicked stuff. If you've got any animals who like to take a stroll in the garden, for goodness sake don't dream of using it. There's no need to either – because there's a perfectly simple way to get rid of weeds in a pathway, by using industrial salt; dendritic salt some of the nurserymen call it. Just sprinkle it on wherever you see a batch of weeds developing and in a few days' time they'll start to turn brown and slowly fade away. You've no worries either about poisoning the animals because if your cat or your dog decides to take a bite at the weeds you've treated, they'll simply taste a bit salty. Nothing worse than that!"

There was never any lack of variety in the correspondence that came Fred's way; but I remember in particular a letter he once received from an elderly lady in Hampshire, complaining ruefully that her apple trees had a grudge against her.

One year they would yield a good crop, producing plenty of apples if not especially large fruit. The following year, when the lady awaited a repeat performance, next to nothing would happen. The trees merely yielded a few miserable 'scrumps' and were scarcely recognisable as the same trees that had given so rich a harvest. "Why", this lady asked, "are my trees treating me so shabbily?"

"Now that's a licker," chuckled Fred. "But I'll tell you this much. It's not the trees that are being unkind to her but more likely the other way round. And he went on to explain to me the wonders and the mysteries of the 'June Drop'. June is the time of year when Nature takes a hand at thinning out the developing apples. She knows that any one tree can only properly handle a limited number of fruit so she takes it upon herself to get rid of at least some of the surplus. For the inexperienced gardener, the sight of all those seemingly promising little fruit tumbling unfulfilled to earth can be a sobering experience – but it is a perfectly natural happening. Unfortunately, Nature isn't always sufficiently thorough; despite the 'June Drop' too many fruit are still left on the tree, and it is at this point that the wise gardener lends a helping hand.

"Wait till the June Drop is over," Fred advised, "then wherever you see two or three fruit in a cluster, thin them down to just one. Far better to have one good apple than four or five scrumps. And remember Frank, if you don't do a spot of thinning you'll very likely get that problem of alternate cropping."

We never heard from the Hampshire lady again so we assumed she had made her peace with the apple trees. But no sooner had Fred given this advice on the air than he was besieged with letters enquiring if the same routine applied to pears. With pears, he counselled, it is wise to thin down to twelve or eighteen inches between fruit; but it is equally important to remember that the pear is a tree with a mighty thirst.

"I remember telling one old chap who lived at Petworth here," said Fred, "that he should soak his pear trees now and again. Next evening I spotted him hopping around the garden with a tiny little watering can, trying to give a huge great pear tree a drink of water. Talk about waste of time; he hardly slaked the poor thing's thirst!"

The degree of watering Fred had in mind for pear trees was in the region of nine to ten gallons a tree; and with lavish treatment on this scale he promised that you were paving the way to some of the juiciest pears you've ever tasted. Like all fruit trees, of course, the pear has its predators. And for those occasions when the wasps or the ants or the earwigs are threatening to taste your pears before you do, Fred had a simple method of keeping them at bay. Tuck a little pad of cotton wool at the base of each fruit so that as the insects move into the attack, they find themselves lost in a barrier of cotton wool. You might imagine that, having crawled unsuspectingly into the trap, they would find it equally simple to crawl out again; but somehow insect minds don't work that way.

Even for the hard-pressed gardener, life brings its little compensations and surely one of the most rewarding moments in the garden comes with the gathering in of the strawberry crop.

"Pick them young before the wasps or the birds can pick them for you," was Fred's advice, remembering always that by keeping the plants well cropped you are giving the developing fruits a better chance to form. 'And when you're actually picking them," Fred added, "treat each strawberry just like Dresden China. Pick them with the stalk of course and never touch the fruit itself because it bruises so easily. Here's another tip too. If you're sending fruit away to someone in hospital wrap each individual strawberry in a leaf or two. That's Nature's own protection you know and it works like magic."

As we saw from his gentle deception of the head gardener at Straffan, Fred could also find magic in the unlovely sight of a pail of manure water. His strawberries were always given two or three dressings of manure water during the period the fruit was developing, taking care of course to dilute it to the colour of a fairly pale ale. Having sampled many a punnet of Fred's Royal Sovereigns I can confirm that they tasted of nothing but strawberry.

"Now I know I'm always saying that every month is a wonderful month in the garden Frank . . . and it's perfectly true," Fred said. "But there's something extra special about July because it's the one month when you can plant any vegetable outdoors with just one exception. And that's celery. Apart from that, you can sow anything your heart desires!"

Most years the soil in July will be pleasantly warm and moist to welcome the seeds; and most years one can count on many more weeks of sunshine and showers to give the seedlings the best possible chance to show their paces.

"They'll grow fast – so they'll grow tender Frank. Get in some more runner beans this month and an extra row of peas as well. And of course you mustn't forget the salad stuff, including another sowing of radishes. The two varieties that do specially well at this time of year are Black Spanish and China Rose. Sow them nice and shallow in the finest soil you can give them; and if you find that they're not developing properly – not swelling out like a good radish should – it's probably because they're not getting enough moisture. So give them a damping over at night whenever the weather's really hot!"

With sound advice like this, Fred pressed home the message that the soil just loves to be busy in July. It is even a good time to plant a few more rows of potatoes – Sharpes Express was the variety he had in mind – so that you can relish the supreme luxury of serving up new potatoes from the garden with Christmas Dinner. How many gardeners have known that joy?

Looking ahead still further (to the following Spring in fact) the prudent gardener will sow in June or early July his antirrhinums and wallflowers and Canterbury Bells for Spring flowering – remembering to sow them sparingly and to wet the soil thoroughly before sowing, not afterwards. Fred would throw up his hand in well feigned horror at the thought that some folk still call the poor Sweet William the 'Stinking Billy'. But his firm favourites for creating the Country Garden ambiance were the Canterbury Bells and wallflowers – and he would urge us to make doubly sure that our selection of wallflowers included plenty of blood reds and yellows, mixed in with the exotically named Persian Market.

"Course, here am I looking ahead to next Spring," Fred admitted, "without reminding you that July is a marvellous month for taking cuttings – and that goes for plenty of the herbaceous plants as well as the ornamental shrubs. Mark you, it's always wise to take your cuttings from really healthy stock and to dip the cutting in a mild insecticide before you settle him in. But I wouldn't be bothered with all those new-fangled hormone dips if I were you. I've taken thousands of cuttings in my time and I've never found them necessary."

Yet the fact remained that many of Fred's listeners quite clearly lacked his green fingers when it came to the taking of cuttings and it was his belief that their failures stemmed not so much from the method of taking their cuttings as from the medium in which they planted them.

"The big thing about the rooting medium is that it must have plenty of air. That's why you want to include a good proportion of silver sand. As a matter of fact, my favourite mixture is three parts sand to two parts of peat and one of loam. Cooor . . . that makes a lovely blend Frank. Don't firm it down too much, otherwise you'll drive out all the air. And don't plant all your cuttings towards the centre of the pot or the box. Put them more around the edges, then they'll get their fair share of air!" Fred was right, as many a thank-you letter was soon to confirm.

Early one August Fred said to me: "I think we ought to talk about making a lily pond. Strange how few gardeners think of including a nice little pond in their scheme of things, yet you don't need all that much space you know."

The broadcast was made and for the next few weeks hundreds of Fred's faithful followers were busily engaged upon miniature excavations in their gardens. Some enlisted concrete for their handiwork; some settled for the prefabricated plastic type of pool. But though the message got home that a gentle oasis of water can add a delightfully restful element to almost any garden, there were also those who wrote to complain that lily ponds soon get covered with all manner of evil-smelling algae and with other weeds that defy every effort to stunt their growth.

"No problem there," said Fred with one of his supremely confident smiles. "They want to get a duck or two on the pond. Those little fellows will soon get rid of the slime."

Fair comment no doubt. But this, I felt, was the moment

to remind Fred that not all his listeners were lucky enough to have ponds in the grand manner and that a family of ducks might feel a shade cramped in a pond only six feet across.

"That's all right," he countered. "They can introduce some goldfish instead. Surprising how the old goldfish will clear up a pond you know! You just try it and see!"

While many of those who worked for Fred in his years as Head Gardener at Petworth will say, with good reason, that he was an unfailingly hard taskmaster, he was constantly seeking ways and means to make life easier for his listeners. He acknowledged, for instance, that even the task of harvesting the blackberries can be an unpleasantly prickly experience; so he suggested that we should all install a few bushes of the Merton Thornless variety in our gardens since (as the name suggests) these are kinder to the hands and clothing and have the added advantage of a long fruiting season. Given reasonable weather they will continue producing a good crop until the end of October.

Picking the blackcurrants can again be a backbreaking assignment and Fred's advice here was to cut out the fruiting branches as soon as the fruit is ripe; the picking of the individual currants from those branches can then be done in the comfort of the kitchen. This not only avoids a great deal of stooping but, in effect, carries out a pruning operation on the bushes. Just a dozen or so new shoots should remain to grow on for the following year.

"Now if you were to ask me," said Fred, "which is the most tricky month in the gardening calendar, I'd probably settle for September . . . and I'll tell you why. You've still got those blessed weeds to keep under control. You've still got plenty of crops to harvest – the potatoes, the onions and the turnips. But now you must keep a weather eye open for the first frosts. And if you've any time to spare after all that, you should be busy potting up your bulbs for Christmas."

It was also around this season of the year that Fred gave special emphasis to the many merits of a greenhouse; not necessarily a large or lavishly appointed house, though he certainly favoured a *glass* house rather than the cheaper variety so popular these days which makes use of transparent plastic sheeting.

"You take the retired bank manager or solicitor," Fred would explain. "He's spent a lovely summer out in the garden and has been saying to himself that this retirement business isn't half bad after all. Then suddenly, as winter closes in, he finds that there's many a day when he can hardly get outside at all. He's like a bear with a sore head – or a fish out of water! So my advice to him is to buy himself a small greenhouse; install a bit of heating if he possibly can – and some lighting too. Then he can potter away in the greenhouse to his heart's content and he won't be getting under his wife's feet all the time."

This indeed was a golden picture Fred painted – a picture of the gardener plodding contentedly down to his little greenhouse, there to discover how his newly rooted cuttings are progressing; and how his out-of-season vegetables are coming along, to give his wife a welcome surprise when the melancholy month of November looks down at her from the calendar.

This was the season too when Fred gave special thought to the army of lonely, elderly ladies who faithfully listened to him each week; and some of them had the strangest ideas about their beloved Mr. Streeter.

One was convinced that although she heard two voices on the radio every Saturday morning – the voices of Frank and Fred – in reality there was only one speaker. Somehow she felt that Fred put on a convincing double act for each broadcast, not only providing the answers to all those gardening questions but voicing the queries as well. Why he should go to such inordinate lengths to deceive her was never quite clear, but none the less she would never miss a broadcast.

It would be wrong to suggest that Fred ever resented the supposed progress of the twentieth century; after all, much of his fame (and some of his money too) derived from media that are as modern as the moment. But on his increasingly rare visits to London in later life, he wasn't much impressed by the city's growing ranks of high-rise flats; and when he turned his thoughts to those listeners who had to live in them, he would picture those dear old ladies entrapped by brick and concrete and gazing down on tired patches of waste ground hundreds of feet below.

"Must be awful Frank," he'd say, "if you've known the peace and the pleasure of your own garden. Then suddenly all you have to look at is four walls. That's why I always say to those dear old ladies – for Heaven's sake get a window-box or two. Then you'll have crocuses and daffodils and hyacinths and geraniums to keep you company right through the year. And don't forget – if money's a bit short – you can even grow a few vegetables in a seed box on the window-sill. Not only mustard and cress which we all know about but a few radishes perhaps and some nice spring onions. With the price of salad stuff these days, it will pay you well you know!"

Letters arrived from those who took his advice, bringing reports on the progress of their window-sill horticulture. Some had tasted radishes for the first time in half a century. Some claimed that their spring onions were more sizeable and more succulent than those to be bought from any local greengrocer. One lady even reported that she was now growing dandelions successfully indoors and that her crops came in earlier than the lettuces and had an interestingly bitter tang in the leaves that put the insipid lettuce to shame. Perhaps the most rewarding letters of all came from those who insisted that the Fred-inspired window-boxes had brought colour to a colourless winter and had lent a note of gaiety to the greyest months of the year.

159

"But don't let anyone tell you that winter is a sad time in the garden," Fred insisted. "I know that by now we should have taken all the frost-sensitive plants out of the ground and stored them safely away in their winter quarters. And I know that by the end of November we should have finished all our digging for the year. But even when we close the door behind us on a winter's evening and say how lovely it is to get snugly into the warm, let's not forget that out in the garden the soil is already preparing itself for another season. What a wonderful thought that is as we slip between the blankets and nod off to sleep on a cold winter's night!"

X

"When I get to the Gates of Heaven and meet Saint Peter, the Gate Keeper, I shall ask – 'Is there any chance of me coming in?' And he'll say, 'What have you been in life?' 'Oh,' I'll say, 'I've tried to be a gardener . . .'; and he'll say 'Come in, come in, come in – we've plenty of weeds up here that want killing.'"

In the opinion of many listeners these were Fred's most memorable words – taken from his most memorable broadcast. The occasion was his ninety-sixth birthday and we were talking together in the Radio 4 programme 'Thought for the Day'.

"Most people," I had said, "are firmly convinced that you, Fred Streeter, are indestructible. But like all of us you're going to die one day. Does the thought of death ever worry you?"

"Not a bit," Fred replied with the conviction his voice could muster so well. "I've had a grand life Frank and I'm looking forward to eternity."

It was then that I asked him to say more about his thoughts of Heaven, and he gave us that glorious glimpse of his meeting with the Heavenly Gate Keeper.

These birthday broadcasts with Fred Streeter were by now developing something of a reputation – and one year later, on his ninety-seventh birthday, when I asked him which had been his most unforgettable birthday of all, he was able to recapture that long past moment with absolute clarity.

It was not some moment of breathless beauty or an occasion of awesome solemnity. Rather typically of Fred, it was an event tinged with humour – at his own expense.

"The year was 1917 and I'd just come back from France – a poor old wounded soldier with everyone fussing round me in that London Hospital. Now when I told them that June 25th would be my fortieth birthday, I was pretty sure there'd be a special treat in store for me. And so there was! The old doctor came along that morning, took one look at me and said: 'We're going to give you a special diet. It's sour milk and castor oil for you my lad!' Talk about birthday treat; that was one and no mistake."

But life's not all castor oil and sour milk and my next question brought Fred a memory with happier overtones.

"Which is the nicest birthday present you've ever received?"

"A bunch of red roses from my wife," he smiled, "with some Penzance Briars . . . those heavenly sweet briar you know."

Then the discussion turned to more practical matters; what would Fred be having for his birthday lunch?

"Probably a few new peas and new potatoes Frank," he said, "but not much meat. Of course, there'll be a cake – I'll have to have a piece of that although I don't go in for rich things much you know. Somehow they don't agree with me."

162

At which point the subject moved again to the matter of age.

"Most of us," I said, "even when we've passed the age of forty or fifty tend to look on our birthdays with rather mixed feelings. What can you say to console us when we feel that the years are really catching up with us?"

"Cooor Frank," he chuckled, "that's an easy one that is. Just say to yourself that every year is going to get better and better. If you really think that way, it's bound to come true – and I promise you, you'll have a lovely time!"

True to his promise, even in his eighties and nineties, Fred was still enjoying a mainly 'lovely time'.

He was still in great demand for radio broadcasts and for the occasional television appearance; and still there were many fête organisers or W.I. secretaries who would write him hopeful letters asking if he could make a personal appearance at some very special event they were organising. Inevitably in those latter years the answer had to be 'no', but it was just such a letter that led me to ask Fred which was the most improbable invitation he'd received since fame had come his way?

"That's a simple one to answer too," he replied. "It was early in 1950 when I received an invitation from a clergyman in Kent. He wrote very nicely, asking if I'd like to preach a sermon one Sunday at Meopham Church because they were holding some sort of festival there. Well remembering I'd said 'yes' when I was first asked to broadcast, I decided to say 'yes' again. But what an experience *that* was."

"A pleasant experience?" I enquired.

"Well I always thought it must be pretty easy to get up and preach a sermon. But I'll tell you this much. Everything looks very different once you're in the pulpit. All those faces looking up at you. And you're just one little fellow looking down at them."

"And what did you preach about Fred?"

163

"Well they'd asked me along because this was the 625th Anniversary of their Parish Church, and they had some pretty important people in the congregation. Even a bishop or so I believe, but never mind. I just told them I was an old Sussex gardener and I reminded them of that line which says 'you're nearer God's heart in a garden than anywhere else on earth!'"

"And how did the sermon go?"

"It seemed to go all right to me," he admitted, "but I'll tell you one thing. They never asked me again!"

If Fred was not born to be a preacher, at least his brand of religion was of a type I could readily accept. He never tried to thrust it upon you, yet it was his guide and his yard-stick in everything he did. And because it was such a simple faith there are many who might say it was bordering on the naïve.

He really *did* talk to his flowers for he was sure they played just as vital a part in the scheme of things as he himself.

He really *did* believe when he went down on his knees and prayed that the attentive ear of God was up there in Heaven, patiently listening to every word he said. And in later years, when he found it difficult to kneel, he admitted to saying his prayers in bed but hoped they would still be judged acceptable.

Sunday by Sunday he would watch 'Songs of Praise' on television and when the weather was fine he would go by car to the village church at nearby Egdean. The church and its Gardens of Remembrance held a host of memories for him since it was here that the ashes of Hilda Streeter were buried. In memory of her he had subscribed the funds for the church's ageing seats to be replaced by a dozen rows of pews in richly polished English oak. His generosity found several expressions in such ways as this — and though the school of sheer necessity had taught him to be careful with money, he believed in spending it on causes he considered to be truly deserving.

He loved the traditional hymns, sung to the traditional tunes. His favourite hymn was 'Love divine all loves excelling.' Church-going for him was always an occasion for the dark suit, the sober tie and the black boots polished to a dazzling shine. But he was never sanctimonious about his faith and never afraid to admit that the same Church he so much respected still had its imperfections.

Knowing that Fred had once preached a sermon himself, I asked him what, in his opinion, were the necessary ingredients of a good sermon.

"Not the stuff that goes into most of 'em," he said bluntly. "Mark you, we're lucky in these parts. Our Rector is one of the best and if I'm ever in need of help I know I can depend on him. He gingers up his sermons with a story or two to illustrate the point he's putting over . . . and that's the whole secret of preaching Frank. Most of us like to hear a well told story and that's where so many parsons go wrong. They send you off to sleep with a lot of high falutin' stuff you can't make head or tail of!"

During the last few years of Fred's life I am sure there were many occasions when he felt the need of spiritual support – and no doubt he said his prayers at such times with added fervency. Yet he also had a useful measure of plain physical courage, as I saw at first hand on one occasion in particular.

On a winter's day in the early 1970's Fred developed a high temperature, lost all trace of appetite and showed many of the classic symptoms of a very old man probably facing his final illness.

Florrie phoned the nearby Petworth Cottage Hospital and soon an ambulance was on its way to take Fred to this little sanctuary he knew so well. True, he was not frequently sick in those latter days – quite the reverse – but he had paid several visits to the Cottage Hospital over the years, either for a brief rest or for the occasional general

165

check-up.

This illness looked altogether more serious. The fever persisted, the antibiotics brought no response; and as time advanced towards the day of our next broadcast it seemed more and more obvious that Fred could not possibly be strong enough to record a programme with me. Yet on the last possible day for making that recording there came a telephone call from Florrie to say that Fred insisted on going ahead with it and could Estelle and I visit the Cottage Hospital the same afternoon.

As we drove along the hedge-lined driveway towards the red brick hospital we wondered how we could possibly pluck Fred back from that cavern of sickness to talk of such earthly matters as parsnip sowing and the digging of celery trenches. How could anyone so deeply committed to a fight for life turn his mind to the trivial battles to be waged in the garden?

The Matron greeted us at the doorway and in her rich Scottish brogue warned us that Fred was very poorly. She doubted if he could muster either mind or voice to make a recording today but if we would wait in a private room she would see what could be done. She returned a few minutes later, wheeling Fred Streeter into the room. He had an almost frightening pallor, his eyes were closed, and there was scarcely a sign of breath in him. If we had been told he had only minutes to live we should have accepted it without question.

Estelle kissed him on the cheek and whispered "Hullo Fred. It's lovely to see you again." There was a flicker of recognition. Then a smile. Then a slow return to a world from which we were sure he was slipping away. He reached out his hand to hers and held it tightly.

I confess I have never been especially easy in the company of sick people. I find the right words hard to come by and I am guilty of a painful awkwardness which can only heighten the tensions the patient himself is feeling. But I did my best.

"We're here for the recording Fred," I said, and at the sound of another familiar voice, Fred brightened further and his voice gained in strength. He sat up in the wheel chair, cleared his throat and dabbed his eyes with a handkerchief. From this moment onwards we were watching the old professional once again turning on his abilities to meet the demands of the moment. Fred was proving once more that he was far from finished.

With Matron observing quietly from a corner of the room we edged our recording equipment near to the base of the chair and I moved close in, to hold the microphone just beneath Fred's chin. His voice would surely be weaker today than was customary; but with a little technique and a lot of good fortune I could probably compensate for this weakness by careful positioning of the microphone.

For the next four minutes I would scarcely have known that Fred was a desperately sick man. He injected that familiar chuckle into his voice and even made a timely joke or two about getting out into the garden despite the harsh weather; and for our sign-off he managed the mandatory 'Cheerio Frank . . . Cheerio Everybody' with almost all of his accustomed vigour. Yet as soon as the recording was over and the microphone had been tucked away, Fred the cheerful broadcaster vanished . . . to be replaced by Fred very close to death. The millions who listened the following morning (though they may have said that Fred didn't sound *quite* his ebullient self) certainly never guessed that this was one of the most courageous broadcasts he ever made.

He recovered slowly from that period of sickness and many more broadcasts were recorded while he was still at the Cottage Hospital in Petworth. We even began to develop something of an affection for the place, and who can wonder? For as winter gave way to an early Spring we would sometimes set up our recording equipment in the summer house deep in the gardens and grew used to the sight of Fred being wheeled across the lawns to meet us, with Matron directing operations.

Arrived at the summer house she would settle Fred comfortably in his chair and then disappear for five minutes or so, to come bustling back with a trayload of refreshments for our little company. Coffee and a plate of cakes (baked in the Cottage Hospital kitchens) for Estelle and for me, and the inevitable glass of blackcurrant juice for Fred.

Once I asked Matron how she rated Fred's health after this latest illness. What were his chances now of reaching that magical century?

"Who can tell?" she replied. "Life is always unpredictable and when you reach that age, the prospects change almost from second to second. But I'll say one thing. Fred Streeter is a very remarkable old man. Anything can happen with Fred."

Happily there were many more golden days still to come and once Fred Streeter had returned to his own home, thoughts of hospital and sickness were soon dismissed from our minds. We started to plan again for the future – and one of our most exciting plans had to do with the broadcast we would make together on Fred's hundredth birthday. There would be champagne of course – plenty of it – and Fred even agreed that he would stretch a point that day and have a little more than his usual perfunctory sip or two. As for the 100th birthday broadcast itself, Fred always said that there were one or two stories about his life that he had not disclosed thus far. If we all behaved ourselves, he might be prepared to tell us those stories on 25th June 1977.

How wonderful it all sounded, and what a memorable broadcast we hoped it would be! But meantime the weekly recordings continued while, by way of excitement, Fred could always count on the occasional visitor from Broadcasting House.

168

John Timpson and Douglas Cameron of the 'Today' programme came to Petworth, insisting that since they had introduced the 'Frank-and-Fred' broadcasts so often on the air, it was high time they met the man who carried the Nation's gardening problems on his shoulders. Another visitor was Michael Aspel who, for all his reputation of knowing the secrets and vital statistics of the most beautiful girls in the world, soon proved that he was equally at home with someone very much at the other end of the age scale.

By the very nature of my job as an interviewer for the B.B.C. I have met hundreds of old people, many of them with remarkable memories and intriguing stories to tell. In particular I recall one old gentleman who described the fate of old age as being rather like that of an elderly railway engine being shunted unceremoniously into some little-used siding and only being noticed when it lets out a plaintive 'peep' on its whistle. Fred Streeter was never shunted into a siding. He stayed firmly on the main tracks, entirely aware of what was happening in the world of the 1970's and especially aware each summertime of the fortunes of Sussex County Cricket Club!

Excitement came when there arrived one birthday a picture of the entire Sussex Team, with their autographs on the back of the photograph and a message hoping that Fred would continue to follow their fortunes for a very long time.

Excitement came in still greater measure almost exactly one year later when a letter arrived for Fred bearing the Royal Crest. It told of the Queen's Award of the M.B.E. to him, and though he was unable to go to the Palace to receive the decoration, this was a gesture which meant a great deal to him, but to which he reacted with the typical question: 'Why an old chap like me Frank?'

Not that this was his only link with the world of Royalty in his nineties. Word reached Petworth that among our unfailing Saturday morning audience was

Queen Elizabeth, the Queen Mother, and when I acquainted Fred with this he gave me a wink and said: "Cooor Frank, we'll have to mind our p's and q's now, won't we? Don't want to get the wrong side of Her Majesty!"

It was always, for me, a fascinating thought that Fred had been around for so long, yet was still such a vital part of the present-day scene. He was born while Disraeli was still in office; he was applying mind and body to the matters and mysteries of the soil long before the Boers laid siege to Ladysmith or Baden Powell sent word to Britain that Mafeking had been relieved. Yet here was Fred, though seemingly spanning great gulfs of time, still equipped to tell the chap in Surbiton why his petunias were a shade off colour . . . still anxious to assure the worried lady in Winchester that the 'June Drop' from her apple trees was a perfectly natural happening.

Sometimes, with our recording session completed, I would sit back in my chair in Fred's kitchen and ask him what he really made of this world of the 1970's. Would he welcome some magical return to the 'good old days' . . . or had he been so closely linked with the contemporary times of radio and television that he felt himself more a product of the 1970's than of his true beginnings back in the 1870's?

"Put it this way," Fred replied. "I don't care much for all these strikes and sit-ins and protest marches we hear about nowadays. Whichever way you look at it, they must be a waste of time. Nothing's ever *made* just by marching down a street shouting angry remarks, and nothing ever gets done just by sitting on your behind saying 'I'm on strike'. But on the other hand, I'm jolly lucky to have lived in this century Frank. Look at the wonderful treatment they've given me up at the hospital. Look at all the miracles the doctors can work. If it hadn't been for them . . . you wouldn't be talking to old Fred Streeter today!"

Sometimes those post-broadcast chats led us into other

realms . . . into the fascinating territory of Fred's own philosophy about Nature in general and Nature as applied to gardening in particular.

"Some people say that Nature is cruel and harsh Frank – and in a sense I suppose they're right, when the winds howl or the snows fall. But as I've said so often, Winter isn't a *sad* time in the garden; the soil is resting then and cleaning itself up all ready for next season; plenty of seeds are already down there, waiting to start germinating; and even when it snows haven't you noticed what a lovely job it does in cleaning the countryside? Not when it's all slushy of course and getting ready to vanish – but when it disappears at last and leaves everything smart and shining like a new pin."

"And here's another thing that may not have struck you Frank. Nothing ever clashes in Nature. You get some posh lady thinking she looks wonderful in her pink blouse and her coat and hat to match. Yet somehow it doesn't come off. Looks awful! But just stop and think what Nature can get away with. Yellow flowers right next to bright red ones. Blue flowers among a mass of green leaves. It all looks absolutely right. Yet that lady wouldn't dream of having a colour scheme like that, not in a month of Sundays! Nature can work miracles with colour – but we poor old humans can't!"

Around this time, however, one of Nature's poor old humans was about to experience something of a miracle; and the man on the receiving end of it was Fred Streeter! For close on two years the sight of one of his eyes had almost completely disappeared. Even in broad daylight he could only detect misty shadows while at night, with just artificial light to aid him, that 'misty old eye' as he called it was neither use nor ornament.

Late one afternoon in Spring Florrie suggested they might take a brief turn in the garden. Remember . . . he was still, in name at least, Head Gardener of Petworth and it

171

was right and proper that he should keep a careful watch on his territory. So Fred planted his trilby on his head at its customary slightly rakish angle, slipped into his highly polished black boots and Florrie drew a coat around his shoulders.

They would make for the sunken garden this afternoon; past the prospering onion beds; past the resurgent fruit trees; past the hot-house where Fred had won so many triumphs. And it was close to this point that the miracle happened.

"Florrie," he said with a mixture of wonderment and disbelief in his voice, "Florrie – you know that misty old eye of mine? I do believe it can see again. Just as good as the other one. It can see again!"

Such excitement there was that afternoon as he cupped first one eye, then the other, to compare the two eyes' capabilities. And there was no mistaking it. The mists had cleared . . . the eye could see again!

On our next visit to Petworth, Fred told me more about that wonderful moment of returning sight. How suddenly the gardens took on new depth, new dimensions. How all at once even the mild Spring colours seemed almost dazzlingly bright. And how, as Florrie and he returned to the cottage, he thought to himself: "It's a miracle and no mistake. Now I can watch my cricket on the television again!"

Fred in his nineties led a well ordered life. He would wake fairly early – no later than six, maybe earlier still – and he would usually be up and about within an hour or so. Breakfast (once a traditional egg-and-bacon cooked meal) was now confined to cornflakes, while lunch, soon after twelve, was frequently Fred's favourite chicken with a potato or two and some lightly cooked greens from the garden. Teatime was almost precisely that; a cup of tea with, maybe, a miniscule piece of cake. As Fred so often said to me, "We old fellows don't need much to keep us going you know. Anyhow, I don't do enough work these days to deserve a heavy meal!"

At the other end of the day, after lending an attentive ear to the early evening news, he would be in bed by seven o'clock with a mug of hot milk and whisky by way of company.

I imagine it is true of most of us that, even with our closest friends, there are certain topics of conversation we instinctively avoid, knowing that to probe them too deeply could bring embarrassment or distress. My conversational no-man's land with Fred concerned children, money, and the many changes that took place in the gardens of Petworth once he ceased to be actively concerned with them.

Fred always said that it worried him not at all that he had no 'cuttings'. Children, he said, might have caused a power of damage to his seedlings and that would never do! He said it with a convincing smile; but I am not so sure that his childless marriage was what he sincerely wished for. He would have made a wonderful father because he had the twin virtues of patience and understanding which are surely the firmest foundations for a happy family.

Certainly there were no insuperable reasons why Fred and Hilda should have had no family; but I suspect that in the early days of marriage their weekly budget was so fully committed that they dared not take on fresh responsibilities. They were careful people, behaving in what they considered to be a responsible manner. Then, by the time Fred rose to Head Gardener status, his life was so much devoted to those particular duties that it would have seemed perhaps a shade disloyal to his employer to change from the dedicated gardener to the family man with divided interests.

Money we never discussed for the best of all reasons: it held little interest for Fred. Stories have been told with the gossipy relish so often applied to matters of finance that gardening never earned him more than five pounds a week; others have put a still lower price on his services, saying that never in life was he paid more than one hundred and twenty pounds a year as a gardener. I don't believe these stories; had they been true, he could scarcely have had over thirteen thousand pounds to leave in his Will. True, this was no fortune; but though he was never affluent in the years I knew him, he certainly qualified for that cosy description of being 'comfortably off'.

"How can you put a price on my job Frank?", he would ask. "You can't place a value on a lovely garden any more than you can plonk down money on the counter and ask Heaven to send us a glorious sunset. But I'll tell you this much. Here at Petworth I've had the best employers any man could wish for. That goes for old Lord Leconfield who was here when I arrived, right through to this very day, with Lady Egremont and her son – the new Lord Egremont. Of course, there've been times when I could have done with a bit more spending money in my pocket. Fourpence a day for that very first job I had didn't leave too much for the luxuries of life; and even one pound a week for my first Head Gardener's job wasn't exactly a fortune. But I made a pretty wise choice you know, and after all I'm still alive to tell the tale!"

In fact – according to the one or two gardeners of his vintage still alive today – Fred *did* make a wise choice by going into 'private practice' rather than into the commercial world of market gardening. He was always sure of a house with a fire in the grate and a front door to close on his private world. He was always sure of an ample supply of garden produce for his table. And with the Leconfield dynasty he elected to serve, he was always sure of the staunchest of allies at times of sadness or distress.

On a more personal note, of all the hundreds of broadcasts we made together, never once did we discuss how much we were being paid for them. So many partnerships these days are based on the admittedly relevant question "What's in it for us?" The Frank-and-Fred team didn't work that way; our only references to finance would come when Fred was perhaps feeling a shade off-colour and I would pull his leg about getting fit again.

"You've got to get well in time for next week's broadcast," I would say. "I need the money Fred!"

He preferred this approach to his health rather than the earnest, solicitous, solemn-voiced enquiry. He liked the brisk assumption that he was still very much a working member of a radio team and that it was up to him to be on form for every appearance.

Yet if money and the lack of children were problems he could cope with, both mentally and materially, I suspect that the one big sadness of his life came with the breaking up of many of the gardens he had created at Petworth. He never questioned the need for these changes because he knew that staff numbers had to be drastically reduced and that, with this reduction, came the need to redesign the gardens for easier working; but it wasn't pleasant to watch.

Just outside his cottage door he saw the rows of familiar greenhouses disappear in sad heaps of broken glass and brickwork, for the land was to be converted into a market garden, selling fruit and vegetables on a strictly commercial basis. These plans did not materialise. Instead a paddock was created here and from his back doorway Fred could now see the playful colts of Petworth sometimes moving at full gallop across the very land where he had raised his gold-medal winning grapes and peaches and nectarines.

As Lord Leconfield once said with good reason: "If all the Gold Medals you've won were *really* gold you'd be worth a fortune Streeter. But since most of them are just cardboard you'd better keep working!"

Fred got the message. And though gardening work in terms of wielding a spade or fork was no longer feasible in his closing years, the changing scene outside his cottage door simply had to be accepted. At least the sunken garden remained a safe and tranquil sanctuary amid all this change, and at least Fred still had his broadcasting to give him an active interest in life.

One change now took place in the routine of our weekly visits to Petworth. Our miniature broadcasting studio in the kitchen was at last abandoned in favour of a cosy spot in front of the dining room fire. Fred was finding it a growing strain these days to sit bolt upright in the high-backed kitchen chair, whereas he could relax in his armchair before the fire, safe from the draughts that sometimes assail the snuggest kitchen and no longer directly within earshot of Florrie's cooking pots.

Despite the domestic cosiness of it all, Fred on his recording days with me was as neat and trim as if he were off to Broadcasting House. He would probably be wearing a grey suit or a colourful cardigan, a dandy blue tie and maybe he would have a woolly blanket over his legs, if the weather was on the chilly side. His thinning white hair would be brushed with an almost military precision; and for all their ninety years of honest toil, his hands would have a manicured delicacy that seemed particularly fitting when he was inspecting some plant or cutting sent in for identification by a listener. Fred with a little known plant in his hands had all the look of the eminent diagnostician in his consulting rooms.

At this period we were recording Fred each Monday, so that if he should be a little off-colour on that particular day we still had the rest of the week to visit him, in time for transmission in the 'Today' programme on Saturday morning. Week after week the formula worked smoothly — so smoothly that our visits to Petworth now had the feeling of an eternal permanence.

The spell was broken one Sunday evening in April 1975 by a very worried Florrie. Fred was showing signs of fever once again and for two or three nights had scarcely slept at all. The doctor was much concerned and had arranged for him to be admitted at once to the Cottage Hospital. There was no hope of our recording tomorrow and the chances seemed slim for the remainder of the week.

Happily we had a number of tapes in hand, dealing with topics not too closely linked to any particular date in the gardening calendar; and the following Saturday our broadcast was prefaced with the comment that Fred was not too well at present but had pre-recorded some sound advice to keep us busy in our gardens.

The announcement had to be made, but the mere hint that Fred was ill brought the expected flood of letters and telephone calls from listeners all over the country. Meanwhile at the Cottage Hospital a virus infection had been diagnosed and they were doubtful whether Fred, nearing the age of ninety-eight, could reasonably be expected to survive.

For the next few days there seemed little hope. Florrie was our messenger, with phone calls morning and evening reporting progress. Whenever the telephone rang outside the expected hour, there was that apprehensive feeling that this could be bad news. These unexpected calls came frequently from the national and local newspapers who by now were keeping their readers informed of day-to-day developments.

But Fred was made of stern stuff. The fever subsided. A hint of appetite returned. And when I telephoned his doctor after the initial crisis had passed, he was able to tell me that once again old Fred had made the seemingly impossible come true. We were not to take this as an assurance that he had regained full health. He was still a very frail old man. But when in mid-April he returned to his Petworth cottage and to Florrie's care, all the sign-posts seemed to say that the next stop on Fred's journey would be that wonderful one-hundredth birthday.

But two or three nights after his return from the Cottage Hospital there came a seemingly trivial mishap, but one with tragic consequences. Fred fell out of bed. He was sleeping now in a downstairs room and Florrie, hearing the bump from her room above, made her way down to his bedside to find Fred dazed but seemingly unhurt in a heap on the floor.

She eased him back into bed, tucked him beneath the blankets and returned upstairs. She had made him as firm and snug as possible, yet still she was strangely worried and could not sleep. She knew that these days Fred was troubled by strange even frightening dreams, some of them taking him back to his days in the trenches in the First World War.

With the coming of dawn came another sound from down below. Once more Florrie made her way down stairs, now to a scene that was far more frightening. Fred had fallen from bed again and was in considerable pain. Easing him back on to the bed was a slow and difficult task. Though Fred could not define the extent of his injuries she knew instinctively that this was something serious and her fears were confirmed when the doctor called early that morning to diagnose the extent of the damage.

Fred had fractured his hip and his femur – severe injuries at any time but desperately serious for a man in his late nineties; at such an age as this, the onset of pneumonia can so often prove fatal. This time when the ambulance arrived for Fred it was to take him not to the familiar Cottage Hospital but to the busy Saint Richard's Hospital fourteen miles away at Chichester. These were strange surroundings where clinical life moves at a pace that can be bewildering to a very old man.

Surely it would not be long before we heard the news we were fearing. But once again the hours gave way to days, the days to a week or so, and although Fred was very weak he was still intermittently conscious. At least the initial crisis had passed.

One afternoon in mid-May, Estelle and I journeyed over to Chichester knowing that a visit to Fred was long overdue yet concerned that excitement could be dangerous.

Fred was not in a private room but in one of the Hospital's main wards. As we were shown into the ward there was an unhappy moment of realisation that he had radically changed from the cheerful old character we loved to a man so frail that he had the merest finger-tip hold on life. At first he did not recognise us at all but sat motionless in a chair beside his bed, his eyes almost closed. Then along the ward came a smiling and briskly efficient young nurse, wheeling a tea-trolley.

"I suppose there's no point in offering Fred any tea," I enquired, more by way of conversation than as a serious suggestion.

"Why not?" she said. "He might enjoy a drink."

She poured a little lukewarm tea into one of those hospital beakers with spout and handle and handed it to Estelle. She offered it to Fred, suggesting that a sip or two might do him good; and to our surprise he was soon accepting it with more than a hint of satisfaction.

There was little conversation that afternoon but merely an unspoken understanding that Fred was in the company of friends. As we left the ward we had a lurking memory of how near to death he looked; and yet we reasoned that anyone who could still enjoy a drink of tea was still very much of this world.

Early in June, Fred came home again. No one suggested that he was fully recovered. Elderly bones do not mend that readily. Yet there was always something about old Fred that suggested an almost superhuman strength; and though now he was spending much of his time in bed, it seemed just possible that a heart which started beating close on ninety-eight years ago might still beat stoically on to that magical century.

There could be no celebrations of course for Fred's ninety-eighth birthday, 25th June 1975. He had few visitors that day although the customary deluge of cards and greetings telegrams arrived to remind him that he was certainly not forgotten. But though many of those cards expressed hope that the dark days of illness were over now, Fred knew beyond doubt that this was to be his last birthday.

That final summer was a spectacular summer in the Sussex countryside. It was as though the flowers and trees were staging their own farewell for him; and as the long, sunlit days gave way to a gentle autumn, the country lanes around Petworth produced a memorable show of gold and copper with all the richness of a Command Performance.

On All Saints Day – November 1st – Fred awoke early. He spoke a few words to Florrie as she tried to tempt him with a sip or two of tea. She remained for several minutes at the bedside and then, as she left, he simply whispered to her "Thank you Florrie" and closed his eyes again.

Late that afternoon the District Nurse called to see her patient. Charles Wales, the Clerk of the Works for the Leconfield Estate, also decided to visit his old friend. For a few minutes they stood grouped around the bedside, then Florrie left for a moment to attend to other things.

There was a sudden call from Charles. It was to say that the end had come with much the same peacefulness that Fred had always cherished in his country gardens. The time was nearly five o'clock. The time most gardeners make for home on a winter's evening.

On a day of quite unseasonable mildness for November, the funeral service for Fred Streeter was held at the Parish Church of Saint Mary in Petworth. It was conducted by the Reverend Guy Furnivall who, for all his short acquaintance with Fred, could already claim one very personal memory of him. Taking Communion with him shortly before he died, he had heard Fred say that, as in the garden, so in life, everything comes right in the end. Nature brings a wonderful calmness as the journey comes to a close.

We were reminded in the funeral address that, in a recorded broadcast on the very morning he had died, Fred had urged us all to have at least one rose in the garden . . . even perhaps a clear, yellow rose of the Fred Streeter variety.

Appropriate words. And appropriate too that a man who, in his quiet way, had so many Saintly qualities should leave the world on All Saints Day; and if Fred's belief has come true, he has tidied the Pathway to Heaven by now and is happily at work in some celestial garden.